GAME, SET AND DEADLINE

Rex Bellamy

GAME, SET

AND

DEADLINE

A TENNIS ODYSSEY

Rex Bellamy

The Kingswood Press

The Kingswood Press
an imprint of William Heinemann Ltd.
10 Upper Grosvenor Street, London W1X 9PA

LONDON   MELBOURNE   TORONTO
JOHANNESBURG   AUCKLAND

Text copyright © 1986 by Rex Bellamy
Photographs/illustrations copyright © by Michael Cole
and Tommy Hindley

First published 1986

ISBN 0 434 98090 0

Printed and bound in Great Britain by
Butler & Tanner Ltd, Frome and London

CONTENTS

The author and publishers would like to thank the following photographers for the use of their photographs:

Tommy Hindley

1, 4, 11, 12, 13, 14, 15, 19, 20, 23, 25, 28, 29, 30, 31, 32, 33, 34, 35, 36, 37, 38, 39, 40, 41

Michael Cole, Camerawork

2, 3, 5, 6, 7, 8, 9, 10, 16, 17, 18, 21, 22, 24, 26, 27, 42, 43, 44

PROLOGUE

THE BLAME for this book lies with the two men who talked me into writing it: Derek Wyatt (publishers' editor) and John Pawsey (authors' 'minder'). They brushed aside the argument that tennis writing was my job; that off-duty literary sallies should refresh the soul with a change of subject. There was no need, they insisted, to produce an entire book fresh from seed. Why not pick a few flowers from the garden of tennis reportage I had been tending for 26 years? After all, the 100th Wimbledon championships would be played in 1986 and we must do our bit to ensure that the mother church of tennis was suitably dressed for the occasion. And (clinching blandishment) was there another British tennis writer on the international circuit with as much regular experience of life at the top?

In fact there is: Richard Evans, an itinerant free-lance. But the persuaders had done their job. I was hooked, but still demurred. With the help of retained cuttings and reference books 75 per cent of the research could be done at home, within hailing distance of wife and Gordon Setter. But readers had always been kind. Why inflict on them such an ego-trip as Bellamy's collected samples? It was then that ideas spilled out of Derek like sand from an egg-timer. Chunks of past reports about exceptional matches and historic 'firsts' could be linked, he suggested, with anecdotes about players and journalists and the fun of the circuit, plus enlightening 'shop talk' about the way tennis reporters worked. In short, I could offer you a broad view of the peaks of tennis as a reporter sees them.

Thus was the fish landed, the contract signed and a fresh supply of typing paper stuffed in the drawer.

What has emerged, I hope, is a book that will be fun to read and will also provide a coherent pastiche of modern tennis history and the players who made it. If there is any literary merit in these pages, so much the better. As I chiselled each chapter into shape it became clear that a few players—Santana, Rosewall, and Panatta among them—had a special talent for enchanting the public as a whole and the writer in particular. But what strikes me most is the way such a leisured stroll through a quarter of a century puts everything into perspective. We are so close to McEnroe and Becker, Navratilova and Lloyd, that we cannot see them clearly— unless they stand, as they do here, on the same wide terrain as Pietrangeli and Laver, Court and King. Even this volume spans only 26 years. The likes of Dan Maskell and Ted Tinling can talk to us about the prime of Suzanne Lengen and Bill Tilden and thus make the perspective even sharper. But the period studied here was one of rapid change and unsurpassed historic interest. Apart from anything else, it transformed a shamateur game into a thriving segment of the world-wide entertainment business.

'Game, Set and Deadline' may be savoured in four ways. First, I have attempted to recapture the character and the quality of great players and some of their matches. Second, many 'firsts' and other oddities are recorded—for example, disqualifications, dope tests, the Wimbledon boycott, the transexual Renee Richards, and 'spaghetti' rackets. Third, the book has been spiced with off-court anecdotes—some familiar, some half-forgotten, some previously unpublished—about the champions and their challengers (and the writing corps, too). There was the evening out that imperilled Margaret Court's grand slam; the time Jimmy Connors needed a loan; the punch that bruised Roger Taylor's knuckles and forced him to scratch from the French championships; and so on. Fourth, there is much here about the life-style of tennis reporters: the excitement of writing against the clock, the recurrent nightmares about communications and deadlines, the pleasures and frustrations of the working day.

Not the least of those frustrations concerns space. Journalists are a garrulous tribe and never have enough column inches to accommodate all they want to write. Even a book poses the same problem. This one is restricted to the three major championships: those of France, Wimbledon, and the United States. Wimbledon, 100 not out, takes the lion's share. I have never been to Australia and had no room to do justice to a variety of thrilling or eccentric events. That great Davis Cup doubles match, for example, in which David and John Lloyd came back from two sets down and saved five match points before beating their Italian opponents at Wimbledon in 1976 ... the day gunfire stopped play at Hampstead ... John McEnroe's match-winning performance in a Fréjus bull-ring ... the joys of Rome and Hamburg, Düsseldorf and Berlin ... Mark Cox beating Pancho Gonzales and Roy Emerson within 26 hours during the first open tournament, at Bournemouth in 1968 ... And my strenuous education in the soccer skills of Raquel Giscafre, Mima Jausovec, and Virginia Ruzici ... Nor is there much here about the sententious intrigues of the game's administrative servants, who tend to regard themselves as its masters.

Reporters are probably the only people in professional tennis who represent none of the game's sectarian interests. We can therefore take a dispassionate view of the passing parade and say exactly what we think of it. Our primary duty is to the readers, rather than to the game or its players. You may reasonably question our qualifications, and it must be confessed that most of us are no better qualified to write about tennis then Bjorn Borg was to win Wimbledon. All that matters is being able to do the job. Basic ability helps, plus hard work and the refining influence of experience. What it boils down to is assembling all the relevant facts in a readable form—to a set length, by a set time.

One has to learn the trade the hard way and in my case the prologue was discouraging. Our headmaster had caned me for cutting the annual prizegiving (I had a date—with a tennis player, as it happened) and he was still peevish when Bellamy of VA was summoned to a terminal interview. Doffing his mortar-board and rearranging his gown, he bleakly studied my scholastic record and then, even more bleakly, me: 'It seems that your talents, such as they are, have been exercised chiefly in writing essays and playing games. I have to tell you that the scope for profitable employment is consequently limited.'

There was only one thing for it: sports writing. And the *Sheffield Telegraph* was looking for likely lads because several senior journalists were otherwise engaged fighting a war. My first tennis report, published in 1949, concerned a public parks tournament in which the runner-up was a man called Kramer (no, not that one). Another coincidence is that Roger Taylor's mother was at that time competing in Sheffield parks tournaments and Roger himself was already 'messing about' at the game, as he puts it. Our paths doubtless crossed, but mine led to Birmingham and London in turn before Roger's tennis blossomed in the public parks of Sheffield.

My own affection for the game was confirmed many years later. Within four days I reported soccer and rugby matches in three seedy, damp and dreary towns. Next morning I flew to Nice, hastened to the tennis at Monte Carlo, dumped my luggage, and sat on the veranda sipping wine. Gonzales and Santana were in action on adjacent courts and sunshine was playing golden games with the sea, the pines, and the craggy extremities of the Maritime Alps. And (you guess?) a great truth dawned: any man who knows what is what, when it comes to the good life, has to write about tennis rather than soccer or rugby. The sunny splendour of the setting was described in lyrical detail in my first paragraph that evening. Whereupon there was a brief silence on the line. Then, back in London, the copy-taker sighed and told me: 'It's pissing down, here'.

The British tennis-writing corps is a microcosm of any closely knit community working under stress and sharing the joys of food and wine and companionship. There are worriers and comedians, malicious gossips and peacemakers, tipplers and raconteurs, womanizers, loners, organizers, those who drift and those who steer— and at any time we can swap roles (to some extent) without loss of camaraderie. Every one merits the cliché 'A good bloke and a good pro' and our overseas colleagues are just as congenial. Ian Barnes sometimes reminds me that when he took over the *Daily Express* job I told him he would be impressed by the high quality of the insults. Nor has he been disappointed.

This book is imbued with the spirit of laughter. All the extracts are from *The Times* unless otherwise attributed. Many of the memories I have taken down from the shelf are yours as well as mine. I have just dusted them over. All I ask now is that you look over my shoulder, enjoy the company, drink the wine, and smell the flowers. We are going to a party. A family party. The family of tennis.

Rex Bellamy

CHAPTER ONE

Paris: Beauty and Pathos

WE USED to talk of the Italian, French and Wimbledon championships as 'the strawberry circuit', because the tennis kept catching up with the fresh fruit as the summer moved north. In the 1960s the peaks of the tournament year stood out more clearly than they do now. For most Europeans the United States and Australian championships were too distant to justify the cost of getting to them. What mattered was Rome, Paris and Wimbledon, in ascending order of importance, and the end of term party in August at the German championships in Hamburg. Those tournaments, plus the Davis Cup team competition, were the scattered summits of the European season—which in turn was the highest massif on the international circuit.

The French championships, the ultimate test on clay (that is, shale), have since advanced in status to share top billing with Wimbledon, the ultimate test on grass. That is as it should be. Paris has always tended to produce the most enchanting tennis of the year, certainly until top-spin became fashionable in the mid-1970s. The artisan excels on clay but so does the artist. Perhaps there is a dash of prejudice, too, in one's enduring belief that Paris is more fun than anywhere else on the circuit. I have French blood, heavily diluted, and was born the same year as the Stade Roland Garros. The name, incidentally, is that of a man who was better known in rugby than in tennis. Roland Garros became a pioneering aviator but was shot down in 1918. He had been a distinguished member of that renowned sporting club, the Stade

Français, who helped to make the new tennis stadium happen—
and they insisted that it bore his name.

One's affection for the French championships has other roots,
too. It happened to be the first grand slam tournament I reported,
at a time when the press telephones were master-minded by the
charming, totally Gallic 'Monsieur Jean', whose slick, steel-grey
hair was no more immaculate than his affability. Transferred
charge calls to London took a long time but Monsieur Jean always
knew where to find his clients. Often he would turn up at the
double while I was watching a match on some distant court:
'Monsieur "Bel-ami". Téléphone!' With luck, a copy-taker would
be free and the line would be good enough to permit accurate
dictation.

Paris is the only city in which I have been afflicted (twice) by a
reporter's nightmare, a jammed typewriter, and the only city in
which I have been tear-gassed (twice, during the 1968 riots). But
the memories are mostly good. Many concern food, wine, and the
company in which they were savoured. Until the late 1970s the
circuit was mixed and a comparatively small troupe of players
and journalists knew each well enough to drink and dine together.
We usually went out in a bunch to some modest restaurant (the
players had less money to spare in those days) but in Paris I also
enjoyed sporadic private 'dates' with Helen Gourlay, Winnie Shaw
and Pat Walkden in an ambiance of wine and candlelight and
chequered tablecloths. We all needed to refresh the soul with a
change of scene. A fortnight at Roland Garros was, and remains,
a tough course to finish. Thank goodness for the secluded calm
of such adjacent haunts as the Jardin des Poètes and, in the Bois
de Boulogne, a little log cabin where simple refreshments are
served.

Journalists need exercise, too. For years a few of us have been
emerging bleary-eyed from our Auteuil hotel for pre-breakfast
jogs in the Bois. And while Shah Jahan was the resident 'pro' at
Eurosquash, in Montparnasse, he would find time to give me an

oil change once a week. Shah gave me 10 out of 10 for effort but once suggested, with mock gravity, that in view of my predilection for wood shots I should not waste money on gut stringing. One day Shah's punctilious regard for the observances of polite society was rudely confounded: moreover, by a woman. I had gone up to Eurosquash with one of the most distinguished figures in Australian squash, Jean Walker. She was playing Shah and behaving like a perfect lady until one muffed shot elicited an explosive ' "Bagger" it!' The shocked look on Shah's face indicated shattered illusions.

It was an Australian lass, Kerry Harris, who told me one year that a women's semi-final in Paris was known in the dressing room as 'The Battle of the Boobs'. Delicacy discourages identification. Nor will I do more than hint at the identity of an eminent and popular player who paid a social call in my hotel room early one morning. I was wearing underpants and pottering about when there was a quiet knock at the door. She was wearing a diaphanous nightie. Manifestly, nothing else. Had this startling vision appeared at the other end of the day, when wine had loosened the bonds of virtue, one might have been reminded that even King David's self-discipline was not impregnable. But I was overwhelmed by apathy at the prospect of adultery before breakfast. And we engaged in small-talk as if that was the only thing either of us had in mind. In her case, perhaps it was.

The character of tennis at Roland Garros, and what it means to me, are summed up in this abridged version of an article I wrote for the magazine *Tennis World* in 1981:

'In the next world, as a reward for distinguished service, we may sometimes be given a day off from stoking duties, or dusting the harps, and issued with the equivalent of Army "leave warrants". Perhaps they will insist, when handing over the travel vouchers (one-day return), that we resume our former, mundane labours. If they do, I shall spend that day at the French Championships—first ensuring that the programme includes matches in which the likes of Pietrangeli, Santana, or Panatta will tease the likes of Laver, Rosewall, and Emerson. If he behaves himself, Nastase can play too. All the matches will last five sets and four hours, even the winners will collapse on the massage table like houses of cards, and I shall miss a few deadlines. But the birds will be singing and the wine will be waiting.

A day at the Franch championships can mirror a lifetime's hope and frustration, beauty and pathos, pleasure and pain. In the past few years the emphasis has shifted slightly away from finesse. But that is probably no more than a passing phase, based on the prevalent dominance of the slickly tailored attritional methods embodied by Bjorn Borg and Chris Lloyd.

The French championships became an international event in 1925 and the Stade Roland Garros was built in 1928. Nowhere else is the grandeur of tennis displayed in such rich variety—and nowhere else is the physical and mental cost of creating that grandeur so cruelly high. In short, Paris is the best place to watch tennis and the toughest place to play it.

Every year, something changes at Roland Garros—but the essentially sensuous pleasures of the tournament remain untarnished. Sensuous? Yes. Because the mind's appreciation of the game is locked in with the sight and sound of tennis at Roland Garros, with the taste and smell of it. With the smell of French cigarettes; garlic; and sun-warmed flowers. With the taste of wine; coffee; crisp French bread; and the inescapable steak frites or sandwich jambon. With the sound of birds singing; umpires nasally intoning *quinze, trente, quarante, égalité, avantage*; and the inimitably soothing slither of shoes shuffling on shale. With the sight of russet-coloured courts amid the grey of concrete and the green of trees, swirling clouds of dust at the mercy of some passing breeze, shirt sleeves and summer dresses in the bright heat of May and June; brilliantly hued crowds on the soaring centre court terraces (like giant rockeries built round a stretch of beach); and line judges dressed in green and grey—among them a chic blonde who flashes just enough leg to remind us that there is more to life than tennis.

Roland Garros has many separate areas of interest, each with its own character and charm. But the centre court sums it all up. It is here that the close rapport between players and public is most exciting. The spectators are cultivated, perceptive. They respond to the mood of drama and players with a passionate, caring, yet discriminating urbanity. At times their noisy enthusiasm threatens to dominate a match by affecting the composure of players and court officials. And in the evenings the echoes of combat rumble on as matches are replayed over dinner—perhaps along the Champs-Elysées, perhaps at some candlelit restaurant in Montmartre, Montparnasse, or the Latin Quarter.

What makes the French the supreme, all-round test of tennis, the most arduous tournament to win, is the combination of heat with a loose, gritty surface that, by means of friction, takes the pace off the ball. The quick-footed, violent cut-and-thrust that prospers at Wimbledon and Flushing Meadow is not good enough for Paris. Rallies last longer. The ball cannot be put away easily. So matches become a prolonged series of tactical manoeuvres containing every trick in the book; every variation of pace and length, spin, angle, and trajectory.

Those sweating, straining endeavours demand both physical and mental stamina. They demand a discreet, concentrated patience on the one hand and, on the other, a constructive alertness to a sudden threat or opportunity. They demand a delicate balance between sparring and a commitment to attack. Openings have to be shrewdly and carefully created—often three or four times in the course of a single rally. Even the superficially simple business of sliding into a shot—so that positioning and balance are perfect—can be desperately difficult unless you have been brought up to do it. And the longer a match lasts, the greater the threat of cramp, shrieking agony, even tears.

A glib analogy between Paris and Wimbledon might be that between a carefully composed classical score and improvized jazz. When watching tennis in Paris, all kinds of images leap to mind: music, geometry, chess, poetry, fencing. Nothing much seems to be happening. Then suddenly, everything is happening—a flurry of punches, perhaps, or the whisper of a drop and the buzz of a top-spin lob. Alarm bells tend to ring in the midst of the most soporific, hypnotic exchanges. Thus the need for mental stamina— the ability to stay alert when everything in you cries out for mental and physical repose.

Watching a match go on court can be like popping a joint in the oven. It can safely be left for a while. You can pop back in an hour or so to see how it's cooking. That was how it was in 1961, when Manuel Santana went to Paris and won his first major championship. He beat Nicola Pietrangeli in a five-set final and was so overcome by the cessation of emotional stress that he burst into tears—and Pietrangeli went round the net, took Santana in his arms, and comforted him like a father calming a child who had woken from a nightmare. That was how it was when, the same year, an Australian teenager called Margaret Smith played in Paris for the first time—and was beaten 7–5 12–10 by Ann Haydon, as she was then. Cramp hit Miss Smith in the second set and the Australian manager, Nell Hopman, dashed on court to help her (in those days, compassion was sometimes allowed to override the rules).

That was how it was, too, in 1969, when John Newcombe somehow produced two aces to beat Jan Kodes 11–9 in the fifth set after more than four hours of an exhausting slugfest. That was how it was in 1972 when Kerry Melville took three hours and 55 minutes to beat Pam Teeguarden (who served for the match four times, had two match points, ultimately ended the ordeal with a double-fault—and sat down and cried). Finally, that was how it was in 1980 when Paul McNamee took four hours and 18 minutes to beat John McEnroe in a match of four tie-breaks: and when Jimmy Connors came back from 3–6 2–6 2–5 and 30–40 down to beat Jean-Francois Caujolle. There had been nothing quite like that since 1958, when Robert Haillet recovered from 0–5 and love–40 down in the fifth set to beat Budge Patty.

It would be an exaggeration to suggest that matches like these are the norm in Paris. But their content was a totally authentic guide to the character of the French championships. How the memories do crowd in—the best of them featuring a subtle clay-court specialist countering the hammer blows of some mighty exponent of the "big" game.

So I'll stoke the fires, or dust the harps. Just get the "leave warrant" ready, and leave the rest to me.'

Back in 1960, when I first reported the championships, the echoing thunder of today's huge crowds was not even a dream. The citizens of Paris hardly knew where Roland Garros was, much less what was happening there. The tournament was essentially a rendezvous for the international family of tennis, especially those with a special affection for clay. And the charm of the occasion did not compensate for the sloppy organization. Players could hang about for hours, wondering when they would get on court—and when they did, there would be no ball boys, probably no line judges, and the blank scoreboards were merely holes in the air. Programmes tended to appear about Thursday. It was as if the organizers slept for 50 weeks, then woke up with a start and improvized as best they could.

The Times was different, too. The piece given here was by-lined 'From Our Special Correspondent' (one of a variety of circum-locutions designed to avoid identifying the writer by name, which was simply not done) and date-lined 'Paris, May 18', the day before publication. It was our practice in those days to specify the dates on which reports from overseas were written. It was also our custom to use initials rather than Christian names when referring to players, and to write of 'lawn' tennis unless discussing the original indoor game now variously known as real, royal, or court tennis.

This 1960 report, which has no particular merit but is liberally sprinkled with half-forgotten names, demonstrates the way generations overlapped (Laver was then 21, Patty 36, and Drobny 38), and serves as an example of the formal style then prevalent on *The Times*. Even in those more leisured days there was sometimes an error in transmission and I have corrected one: Bungert's cross-court volley somehow became a 'squash court' volley. I was too raw to risk more than a hint of technical analysis but the comments on Knight indicate that, even during this callow period, I was developing an appreciation for a player's appearance, personality, and court presence. A newspaper's readers are not all mad about tennis but all are interested in people. The specialist reporter who preaches only to the converted is not doing his job properly.

'The Stade Roland Garros was in a quieter, more business-like mood for the second day of the French lawn tennis championships. For Britain it was a case of one step forward and two back— W. A. Knight won but J. E. Barrett, captain of the team, and Mrs R. Hales both lost—yet on a broader canvas there was much to talk about among the rustling trees as the seeded players ran into trouble.

The only one to lose was J. E. Lundqvist, who retired after losing the first two sets to D. W. Candy. Lundqvist and his Swedish compatriot, U. Schmidt, have just finished a Davis Cup tie and that it had left its mark on them was clear from the way both went out today. N. A. Fraser, another seed, dropped two sets to J. M. Couder amid the soaring terraces of the centre court, and Knight and N. Pietrangeli were other seeds who needed more than straight sets to get through, Pietrangeli for the second day running.

But all this faded into relative insignificance as A. Licis gave R. Laver, last year's runner-up at Wimbledon, a formidable test as the evening's first soft shadows fell across the court. Laver is seeded fourth here, but with a match point against him at 2–5 in the fifth set all seemed over. Incredibly he not only saved that point but with some new fire of inspiration burning within him fought back to level terms and finally to victory by 2–6, 6–8, 6–4, 6–3, 8–6.

Another Australian in adversity was R. Hewitt, their number four, who lost to I. Buding after a stirring first set. R. Mark, too, Australia's number five, lost his way against R. W. Barnes, of Brazil, after winning the first two sets. But if Australia had a bad day Brazil had a good one, for Barnes and C. Fernandes both got through, the latter earning a match with Britain's R. K. Wilson tomorrow. Knight will oppose J. Ulrich.

Knight took just over an hour and a half to beat W. Bungert, the German Davis Cup player, by 6–8, 6–2, 6–3, 6–2. As the score suggests, it seemed at one time that Knight was in for a much harder and longer match. Bungert was the more composed of the two—which will surprise no one who knows his Knight—and won many points with a smoothly played cross-court backhand volley. He had, too, a good first service and a powerful forehand which often took Knight by surprise when played from deep in defence. In addition, he frequently kept Knight quiet by pegging down the left-hander on his relatively weak backhand.

As for Knight, he often wore the look of a man whose creditors were closing in. Towards the end of that first set particularly, it seemed that every point was a crisis in his life. But there was ample evidence of his experience and inner coolness in the way he left alone many a shot that a less mature player would have taken before it had a chance to go out. Once on top he never relaxed his grip on Bungert or himself, and after the first set the German had to gather what crumbs he could from the rich man's table.

But in the first set Bungert was at his best and Knight was not. Each lost his second service game, Knight almost but not quite achieved a break-through in the tenth, and the break that mattered came in the 13th game, Bungert then holding his service for the

set. The grapevine here is as efficient as it is elsewhere, and
spectators came flocking in as Knight set to work to balance the
books. Uncertainty was behind him now—some men are happiest
with a load on their backs—and Bungert found him irresistible.

The second set contained the finest rally of the match, but
Bungert had his back to the wall and—with light rain threatening
an interruption—Knight won the last three sets in a trice, acing
Bungert on the only match point that was necessary. The quick
kill did not suit everyone, however, for an Englishman who had
watched Britain's Davis Cup tie in Holland, and had then walked
to Roland Garros, arrived hot foot in time for no more than the
final handshake. But he was philosophical about it—there was
plenty to see elsewhere.

On other courts two distinguished old-timers received the coup
de grâce and, sandwiched between them, J. N. Grinda was making
short work of P. Jalabert in a match of much local significance.
There was a touch of sadness in the sight as most of the spectators
crowded round the French pair while on the flanks, as it were, J.
Drobny and B. Patty were yielding to the years and to J. Brichant
and M. Llamas respectively.'

The Laver–Licis match deserved more comment but obviously
finished late in the day at a time when my piece had already been
written. All I could manage was a brief interpolation. André Licis,
a Polish Davis Cup player, was hot stuff on clay. He never won
much but he took a long time losing. Licis was only 5ft 4½in tall.
'I am zee smallest', he told me, 'but I run quick'. In many ways
he was typical of east European clay-courters: a breed vividly
summed up by Abe Segal, one of the most colourful, down to
earth characters ever to enliven the courts. 'You hit the hell out
of the ball and they still put it past you', said Segal. 'These guys
are so fit and strong. They're built like fucking tanks and they run
like deer. Give 'em a smell of the boddle and they're off. They
should be entered in the Grand National.'

The modest paragraph about Laver and Licis is a reminder that a reporter who can watch a day's play and then sit down to describe it at leisure is lucky indeed. Given, for example, the task of writing 600 words, one often shifts 400 by later afternoon, reserving 100 each for a 'top' and 'tail' to be sent late when the overall pattern of the day is manifest. A 'top', 'intro', or 'nose' (the French call it a 'chapeau') is the beginning of the finished report and the 'tail' the end of it. But in *The Times* of 25 years ago one could get away with a flowery intro, uncluttered by hard news, that merely set the scene. This example, dated May 17, 1961, was embellished by news of peripheral difficulties, by an imaginative French translation of Eugene O'Neill's then fashionable play *The Iceman Cometh*, and by a suggestion that Rod Laver (of all people) was developing a knack of finishing second:

'This morning, with posters in the Latin Quarter ominously announcing "Bientôt Le Yeti", there were no Metro trains, no buses, no electricity, and here at Auteuil still no programmes for the French lawn tennis championships. Transport or no, the crowds came streaming to Roland Garros as the sun smiled on another gusty, dusty day.

The artists with their paint brushes had to dip into their third different colour for the immaculate mural of results. Ten men took their places in the last 16 of the singles, among them the top seeds, Pietrangeli, champion here for the past two years, and Laver, who is anxious to shake off a growing reputation as a runner-up.'

That same report contained an accurately prophetic comment about Mike Sangster, the only British player since Fred Perry to reach the semi-finals of the Wimbledon (1961), United States (1961) and French (1963) championships. It came after a reference to Jan-Erik Lundqvist's win over John Barrett, captain of the British team in Paris:

'Happily Sangster, on the adjacent court, was showing us that he may soon earn a place in the upper strata of the game. It is a measure of his growing stature that he dropped only seven games to the tall Stolle, a determined, promising player who gained a place in Australia's official overseas team after a consistent summer at home.'

The two singles events were each down to 16 when 'the programmes burst upon us this evening with the twilight chorus of birdsong'. But in those days that was par for the course, much less significant than the first appearance of an Australian who was to achieve even more renown than Fred Stolle. Margaret Court was to win more grand slam championships than any other player of either sex. But in 1961 she was still learning her trade, especially on the slow clay courts of Paris, when she met Ann Jones. Miss Smith and Miss Haydon, as they were then, met on May 23. The match is described in this extract, via syntax that sometimes suggests the players were in better form than the reporter:

'Miss Haydon beat the 18-year-old Miss Smith, twice Australian champion, by 7–5, 12–10 in an absorbing and increasingly tense test of mental and physical stamina that kept them on court for almost two hours of a sweltering afternoon. The finish had a note of sadness, for when Miss Haydon led 7–5, 10–10 and 15–0 on service, Miss Smith, suddenly crying quietly, had to stop because of cramp in her feet. Within three minutes she was ready to continue the ordeal but she lost the game, and, after taking salt tablets, the next also after saving two more match points—she had already saved three in the 20th game.

Here was a fine performance by Miss Haydon against a player who, on her first tour of Europe, had previously only been beaten by Miss Bueno, whom she had earlier defeated in Australia. Tall and athletic, Miss Smith bases her game on the serve and volley. Today she showed good judgment in timing her advances to the net, often after a dipping backhand approach shot, and put the ball away with almost masculine competence. She rebuffed many of Miss Haydon's own advances with good passing shots, and had no glaring weaknesses which the British player could exploit.

In the face of this formidable challenge Miss Haydon needed all her experience. She fought every inch of the way and varied her game skilfully when it mattered most, her drop shot gaining many a valuable point. In the first set she led 3–0 but was pulled back to 3-all and game after game hung on a thread until Miss Haydon reached 6–5 on her fourth game point and then broke through for the set. In the second each player again won three games in a row. Miss Smith had a set point in the 18th game but, perhaps nervous at the crisis, served a double-fault and lost the chance. Then she in turn was fighting desperately to get out of the pit and as it happened the strain was more than she could stand.'

In November of 1953, while working for *The Birmingham Gazette*, I reported a table tennis international in which Miss Haydon, a local girl 24 days past her 15th birthday, won both her singles. The first turned the tide in England's favour and the second ensured victory over Hungary. Miss Haydon moved over to tennis, I moved over to *The Times*, and for more than a decade her distinguished career gave me plenty to write about. We shared a little laughter on the way, and still do. Those 1961 French championships were landmarks for both of us. Miss Haydon won her first big title and I reported the finals of a grand slam tournament for the first time.

Miss Haydon did better in her metier than I did in mine. True, her triumph was big news for any British newspaper. But I should have done more to capture the thrilling emotional impact of the scene at the end of the men's final—with Santana in tears, Pietrangeli gently taking the Spaniard in his arms, and the huge crowd responding to an embrace that was at once both public and private. This is an abridged version of the published report:

'The respective sixth seeds became French lawn tennis champions here yesterday. In the case of Miss Haydon of Britain this was no great surprise. Her break-through to the top was only a matter of time. But nobody would have predicted that Santana, the little, boyish-looking Spaniard, would beat the top three seeds in ascending order—Emerson, Laver and Pietrangeli. Yet these two young players (Miss Haydon is 22, Santana 23) have now gained their first major championships.

As Miss Haydon and Miss Ramirez were formally presented by the umpire, it seemed that the British girl was the less at ease. Her first tentative drop shot was returned as a winner. Almost before she had started she was down 0–2. Still, at this first scent of danger her fighting heart stirred her to attack, just as it had done earlier when she was in a perilous position against Mrs Kormoczy. Suddenly, without warning, she became "l'agressive Britannique" as she has been called here. Confident, on her toes, she was playing an assertive, all-court game, admirably controlled, with drops and lobs measured to an inch.

The crowd roard their admiration and encouragement. Nevertheless, one's heart almost stopped as time and again she went to the net without, it seemed, sufficient cause. But Miss Ramirez, intimidated, could not produce the passing shot or lob demanded. Quickly she became confused. When she went forward she was passed or lobbed, when she stayed back even her length deserted her. Mistakes flowed from her racket as the initiative passed completely and irrevocably from her. From 0–2 down, Miss Haydon won six games (gaining the last 12 points of the first set), lost one, then took the next six for the match.

Though this, in a sense, was a one-sided anticlimax, the men's final was a complete contrast, with Santana and Pietrangeli each stepping from light to darkness in turn as the match followed its curious course. Santana won by 4–6, 6–1, 3–6, 6–0, 6–2. And as the last point of all was tucked away, the Spaniard's nervous control cracked at last and, suddenly, he was sobbing quietly.

It was a moment of unbelievable triumph for the frail-looking Santana, who used to be a ball boy at a club in Madrid. The prize was richly deserved. In spite of his occasional nervousness he did not let the occasion spoil his natural game. Here again were his subtle variations of pace, spin, length and angle, delicately caressed drop shots and lobs. Often Pietrangeli matched and even mastered him as they fenced for an opening, but the Italian was never at his best for long.

There were times when he made the game look absurdly easy, when Santana's strokes were drawn to his racket as if by magnetism, when the Spaniard's keenest thrusts were countered by winners. But Pietrangeli's rhythm was broken up by Santana's flickering subtlety, and the dying fire of his own inspiration had no flame to offer as the wind of defeat grew ever colder.'

On May 20, 1963, the unseeded Sangster became the first British player to reach the men's singles semi-finals since Bunny Austin in 1937. This was almost as gratifying for British reporters as it was for Sangster. But wider historic horizons had already been explored, as was noted in this extract written on May 16:

'Then came a scandal that made the swarming spectators unusually talkative, even by French standards. It will go down in the game's history as a cause célèbre, for here was what is believed to be the first case of its kind, a player's disqualification because his conduct prevented play from being continuous, as it must be according to the laws. The victim was Alvarez, of Colombia, often a controversial figure. His opponent was Mulligan and, to make the whole thing more embarrassing, the umpire, like Mulligan, was a young Australian.

Alvarez frequently held up play by disputing line decisions and Mulligan once made a move to walk off court but was induced to carry on. Alvarez had already been warned before he was finally disqualified by a delegate from the tournament's management committee. At the time he was leading 7–5, 4-all. The arguments that went on afterwards were many and various. Some took the view that the decision was necessary and just, others that a character like Alvarez makes the game more fun. But a stand has to be made somewhere, sometime. Players everywhere know now that a precedent has been set, that even in the absence of line judges the umpire's word has to be accepted.'

The news may have seeped through to Bucharest and the 16-year-old Ilie Nastase. But we may assume that John McEnroe, aged four, was not yet in the market for anything more sensational than picture books, the alphabet, and nursery rhymes. A decade and more was to pass before each in turn raised the ghost of Willi Alvarez and 1963.

The 1964 singles finals produced some classic tennis. Miss Smith beat Miss Bueno and in the men's event Santana and Pietrangeli were at it again. This time I did them more justice:

'For more than two hours the smouldering arena throbbed with passion and artistry as Santana and Pietrangeli, making us all feel three years younger, reenacted the final of 1961. That was the first time any Spaniard had won an important championship, and at the end Santana cried in Pietrangeli's arms. Paris had not forgotten that moving scene.

Yesterday, these eloquent Latins again played a match that was all subtlety and wit. Again Santana won—by 6–3, 6–1, 4–6, 7–5. Again the umpire had to ask an enraptured crowd to be quiet during the rallies. Twice, Pietrangeli spread his arms in mute appeal after muffing a shot during a sudden explosion of applause. Santana once held up his left hand to induce silence while his right was poised to put away a short lob.

Santana and Pietrangeli responded to the occasion, to each other, and to the crowd as everyone knew they would. Neither is cold inside. They played as much from the heart as from the head.

In their hands the game became a thing of beauty. Paris is an annual reminder of the craft and culture tennis can command and here was the world's finest hard court player, Santana, laying out his store of riches at the prompting of a perfect foil.

Santana, 26, is at his peak. Pietrangeli, 30, is beyond it. He hardly ever trains and rarely goes to bed before one o'clock. If he went to bed early, he says, how would he occupy the mornings? Yet Paris always strikes a chord within him, for here the artist is king. This was his fourth French final in six years and in reaching it he beat the Australian and Italian champions, Emerson and Lundqvist.

Yet now, for almost three sets, Pietrangeli was in the shadows. Santana, serving admirably, had a string of aces and service winners. His forehand was superb, his touch gracious and assured. His game was at once versatile and consistent, intelligent and imaginative. He led 6–3, 6–1, 4–2 and even had a point for 5–2. Then, with victory only a few minutes away, his concentration wavered, his confidence faded.

Pietrangeli exploited his reprieve by winning six games in a row. The crowd, eager to prolong their pleasure, bore him along on a surging wave of encouragement. Now it was Pietrangeli, not Santana, who had the confidence to conceive winners and the accuracy to play them. At 5–3 in the fourth set Pietrangeli had five set points on Santana's service. At 5–4 he served for the set but lost the game to love. His chance had gone, for Santana, attacking anew as his concentration returned, was now revealing his finest qualities as a competitor.

But Pietrangeli was still playing well. Previously each in turn had held the stage. Now they held it together in a glorious climax, with four match points to prolong the delicious agony. Then, at last, Santana was home and the heat and the noise throbbed around them for the last time. They raised their arms to the heavens. They embraced, as they had done three years earlier. Again they had fashioned a match of consistent charm and frequent splendour and, in its making, they had again taken pleasure and given more.'

(The reference to 'hard' courts is old-fashioned and confusing. Usage has changed. Today's 'hard' courts are grit-free. Courts with a loose top dressing, as in Paris, are known as 'clay' or 'shale'.)

Bob Carmichael, a brawny Australian who answers to 'Nails' because he used to be a carpenter, has considerable shoulders that seem to govern every lurching movement. He has the mien of a tragedian and speaks volumes with no more than a twitch of the eyebrow or the kissing muscles. When Carmichael does utter, his voice is a deep, resounding rumble. Other players always went to watch him—to watch Carmichael, that is, rather than his tennis, which was homespun and careworn. But Carmichael had his days and in 1967 he made a special effort to prepare for Paris. For two weeks he 'worked out' with Roy Emerson, which would ruin most men. Carmichael ran, exercised, practised. He did all the right things. And in the first round he was beaten in straight sets on the centre court by somebody called Ichizo Konishi, from Japan. 'I'd never been so fit', Carmichael told me later, 'and I had a good draw. But I couldn't play ...' Carmichael's bearing, mind you, always implied that when nothing could go wrong, something would.

Emerson beat Tony Roche in the final that year. After the match I hurried away with Barry Newcombe of the *Evening Standard* to watch France play Russia at football. In a few crowded hours we saw some incredibly fast reactions at the net—first Emerson's, then those of Lev Yashin, the Russian goalkeeper. But that year at Roland Garros is best remembered (certainly by the French) for a heroine rather than a hero. This is the way I put it:

'French tennis will long remember this sweltering Sunday afternoon. At 4.20 the crowded centre court of the Stade Roland Garros—its four vast banks ablaze with colour, like giant flower-beds—almost burst asunder with noise and movement. France was saluting its first women's singles champion since Nelly Landry (French by marriage) in 1948 and its first French-born winner since Simone Mathieu in 1939.

The new national heroine is Françoise Durr, born at Oran, Algeria, on Christmas Day, 1942. Already she had dismissed Maria Bueno (Brazil), the United States champion. Today she beat Lesley Turner (Australia), the Italian champion, by 4–6, 6–3, 6–4 in an arduously close match that lasted for an hour and 35 minutes.

Miss Durr's triumph was a smack in the eye for the purists, a vindication of all those who claim that character is more important than talent, and a sharp rebuttal of the silly old cliché that nice guys—or nice girls—finish last.

Miss Durr's sunglasses and her pink hair-ribbon are distinctive but not elegant. The same applies to her grip and her strokes: especially the sliced backhand that often takes her down on one knee. What binds all the peculiarities together and makes her such a bonny competitor on hard courts is her ball control, the result of painstaking hard work, and the unfailingly sharp wits that command her tactics. She knows where the ball needs to go for maximum effect: and she has the control to put it there.

The crowd's collective heart was at one with Miss Durr's. Even while rallies were in progress, there were shrieks of joy or gasps of horror. How she had to fight! At 6–4 and 2-all Miss Turner looked well on the way to regaining a title she had won twice before. In the third set, marred by the distraction of controversial line calls, she came within two points of leading 5–2. But Miss Durr caught her, then pressed an attack on Miss Turner's backhand. This squeezed out a last, decisive error, at which Miss Durr flung her racket so high that it might have brained her on the way down.'

The 1968 French championships were the first grand slam event to accept full-blooded professionals as distinct from the shamateur breed. Legendary figures were back in the family. During the preceding week, on the same courts, the women contested the world team championship for the Federation Cup. But that was also the time when riots and strikes were threatening Paris with anarchy. Getting there was an adventure in itself, because all flights and trains had been cancelled. Early one morning, in a Roman hotel at the end of the Italian championships, I made 13 telephone calls in an effort to solve the transport problem—and came up with a scheme that might just work. Virginia Wade, the last British player left in Rome, was thinking on similar lines and we decided that two might cope better than one.

We squeezed onto a packed flight to Brussels and there collected provisions, Belgian and French currency, a hired car (with a full tank), and two more passengers—those charming Finnish blondes, Birgitta and Christina Lindström, who had never played in Paris before and had begun to suspect they were not going to make it this time. I was short of sleep and feeling jaded. Amid all kinds of nasty rumours, one to the effect that petrol stations were closing, the idea of driving through a disordered France with three young women was slightly worrying.

But Miss Wade, bless her heart, shouldered more than her share of the Brussels chores and the driving—and shortly before midnight the lights of Montmartre appeared on the horizon. The trip went like a dream. 'I enjoyed it,' said Miss Wade. 'I'm all for a little bit of fun.'

Thank goodness it amounted to no more than that. Come to think of it the trickiest bit, after the girls had been distributed elsewhere, was finding somewhere to park in those narrow, congested streets around the Place St Michel. My hotel happened to be slap in the middle of the riot area and in the nights to come I spent sleepless hours coughing the tear gas out of my lungs and, once, was helplessly caught in the middle when students and police set about each other. There was nowhere to go so I took notes and, next day, wrote a little feature about it. That trip from Rome to Brussels and Paris had also given me the chance to file stories from three capital cities on consecutive days.

Ken Rosewall, who flew in from New York and landed at a military airfield, was the first 'promoter-controlled' professional to arrive. There was not much petrol available in Paris and on the first day of the championships the bearded Torben Ulrich, philosopher, musician and jazz critic, had a rucksack on his back when he turned up at Roland Garros on a borrowed bicycle. Nancy Richey asked me anxiously: 'How do we get outa here?' Word had got around that I knew a former racing driver, the friend of a friend, who had access to petrol. But Miss Richey stayed and was glad she did. She and Rosewall became the first grand slam singles champions of the open era.

The press room was exciting. 'Monsieur Jean', looking unusually serious, soldiered on for a few days in spite of union pressure but was then sucked into the strike. But Barry Newcombe, always a DIY expert when it comes to telephones, tinkered with the magic box until he got the hang of it. After that we put through our own calls to London. Unpleasant though it was in some ways, the ambience of Roland Garros was thrilling: and the crowd figures soared to unprecedented heights because the professionals were back, the sun was shining, and the strikes left Parisians with time on their hands. The tennis caught the mood, especially during the first weekend:

'The centre court of the Stade Roland Garros has glittered with enchantment these past two days. The vast amphitheatre has smouldered with heat. Its steep banks, tightly packed with spectators in summer colours, have been a dazzling sight. The players must have felt like ants, trapped at the foot of a giant rockery in full bloom.

With its blend of sharpness and subtlety the tennis matched the setting in both character and quality. The professionals, used to playing indoors, looked at the brightness and beauty around them

---

and felt, perhaps, that such gloriously 'open' tennis as this was made for the gods.

Appropriately, the professionals kept their dignity, though some were challenged by players who, for part of a match, were able to lift their games to the same level. This was true yesterday of Herb FitzGibbon, an American, who played so well that he had Ken Rosewall in a corner at one set all and 5–1 in the third.

Rosewall played wonderful tennis then, saving three set points and almost stopping the heart with the lashing facility of his ground strokes. There were puffs of dust as the ball bit into the court like a bullet. The mighty crowd made thunderous noises— and then fell back into intimidating multitudinous silences.

Today it was the turn of another American, Cliff Richey. At one set all he took Roy Emerson (the reigning champion) to 14 games in the third set and then 20 in the fourth—for which Richey had a set point. Yet the hard opposition of FitzGibbon and Richey became but shadows in the memory as Ricardo Gonzales today exposed the richest texture of his game in beating Istvan Gulyas by 6–4, 6–2, 6–2.

This was an extraordinary result because the little Hungarian, runner-up here two years ago, was expected to tax Gonzales to the full and possibly beat him. But Gulyas, a modest man, did not fancy his chances against a net-rushing professional. Perhaps, in a sense, this was a clash between a big man and a small man.

In any case Gonzales today made tennis look the loveliest of games. He was efficient but he was romantic. His serving and smashing was explosive. His ground strokes, stop volleys and drop shots had the delicacy of feathers blown by a gentle breeze. At times he seemed to have too much respect for the ball to hit it hard. Instead he whispered to it, like a fond parent lulling a child to sleep. To watch Gonzales was to think in terms of poetry and music. He did not play the game. He composed it.'

Gonzales, already 40, inspired more imagery when he beat

Emerson in a five-set match spread over two days. I suggested that the last two set 'linger on the palate like good wine', that Emerson covered the court 'with predatory, cat-like grace', and that 'many of the rallies were as finely woven as some gorgeous tapestry'. Rod Laver's education was advanced when he came back from nowhere in particular to beat the lumbering, lunging, leaping Ion Tiriac, a cunning player with an arresting, intimidating personality. There was a time when Laver was being jerked to and fro 'like a puppet on a string. He was running in circles. His legs were getting mixed up'. During this phase 'he was playing the game from memory in a strange world that recognized none of the conventions of his own', I included all but one word of this remark by Laver: 'The ball was coming at me 20 ft high. I felt like catching the bloody thing, throwing it back, and saying "Can't you do any better than that?" '. In those days *The Times* was gradually overcoming its reluctance to publish comments made by players.

By 1969 a new regime had taken over French tennis, the changes including a short-lived experiment with floodlighting on the centre court. That was the year, too, when Roger Taylor had to scratch because the knuckles of his racket hand were bruised and swollen—the consequence of punching the hard-headed Bob Hewitt in a Berlin dressing room. One day I wrote a piece that said much about the character of the championships. Most of it is worth another airing:

'All the beauty and drama of life, all its passion and pathos, were mirrored in the small world of tennis here today. The enchantment of the French championships, the game's greatest test of all-round ability, settled upon us like a strange and lovely dream. On waking up, we found that both singles events had been reduced to eight.

First, the pairings we shall examine when battle is resumed: Tony Roche v Zeljko Franulovic, Ken Rosewall v Fred Stolle, Tom Okker v John Newcombe, Andres Gimeno v Rod Laver;

Billie Jean King v Lesley Bowrey, Ann Jones v Rosemary Casals, Julie Heldman v Nancy Richey, and Kerry Melville v Margaret Court. That list includes eight former champions, four in each event.

There was a great match today—played on a new "show" court tucked away among the trees by a children's playground. Newcombe, already champion of the German and Italian clay courts, beat the 23-year-old Jan Kodes of Prague by 6–1, 6–4, 0–6, 8–10, 11–9. In the fourth set Newcombe had an early break and served for the match at 7–6. In the fifth Kodes led 4–1, had two points for 5–2, and was twice within two points of winning.

Somehow, at the end of it all, Newcombe managed to summon the strength for two pulverizing blows—service aces that won him the match from 10–9 and 30–15. He said afterwards that he hit the first ball as hard as he could and the second even harder. "That's one of the toughest I can remember, especially the finish." He talked as if in a dream, and as he talked this young superman sank onto the massage table, as drained as a Samson whose Delilah had turned sour on him.

For pathos, there was Manuel Santana of Spain, playing his compatriot, Gimeno, for the first time in nine years. Santana's game shone in its full splendour: all light and loveliness, caressed by the most delicate brushwork. Even the gifted Gimeno was made to look like a craftsman enmeshed by baffling artistry. But at the crux of the third set Santana pulled a groin muscle and at 0–1 in the fifth he retired.

In the dressing room Santana, crumpled and broken, sat on a bench with his head on his hands. Newcombe did not so much lie on the massage table as collapse on it. Kodes, his slim, whipcord frame sapped of strength, hid his private pain behind a grim mask that told us nothing, yet everything. What a cruel game tennis can be! But all this was for the public's pleasure on a day that smouldered with heat. The mighty centre court was suddenly crowded and colourful and emotional after two rainswept days.

Okker, all tiptoe brilliance, frustrated that tough, brave little Texan, Cliff Richey. Franulovic and Stolle respectively swept past Roy Emerson (who looked as if he had been on clay too long) and Arthur Ashe (who looked as if he had not been on clay long enough). Rosewall and Laver played like the masters they are ...

The whole weekend, indeed the whole game, was summed up by the contrast between, on the one hand, the crowds and the applause, the sunshine and the drama, and—on the other—the quiet pain in the men's dressing room as the birds sang their last chorus of the day.'

Such a picture in words could not have been painted without access to the touching scene in the dressing room. In those days there were fewer reporters and the players knew who they could trust. But the reporting corps multiplied and turned up in anonymous droves—and some were none too scrupulous about what they picked up in the dressing room. Eventually the press were barred. The report you have just read could no longer be written.

One of the best kept secrets of 1970, when Margaret Court completed a grand slam of the Australian, French, Wimbledon and United States championships, was her sickening Saturday in Paris. She won her semi-final on the Friday and had a day's rest ahead. That Friday evening Margaret, her husband Barry, Pat Walkden and I made up a foursome at a little restaurant in a back street off a back street near the Place St Michel. We ate well but discreetly and, as I remember, had only one bottle of wine between us. In retrospect, I may have erred in recommending the champignons à la Grecque for starters. Later we paused at some pavement table for a contemplative beer: and a French passer-by, presumably in the medial phase of getting plastered, studied Margaret's sandals at length and announced gravely that she had the most beautiful feet he had ever seen.

Other than that bizarre incident, the evening was pleasantly uneventful. In terms of food and drink, seemingly harmless too.

Next day Margaret and Barry did not show up at Roland Garros. On the Sunday she beat Helga Niessen in an awfully tiring final played in ferocious heat. I typed and telephoned my report and then went next door to the bar, in the sure knowledge that such good Australians as Margeret and Barry would be sinking a few celebratory beers. It was then that Barry broke the news:

'Margaret was crook all day yesterday', he said. 'And I mean crook. I was digging the stuff out of the sink with a coathanger. If she'd lost the final we weren't going to tell you—no fault of yours, mate, but we knew you'd feel bad about it.' How's that for tact? But thank goodness Margaret won the final and, later, wrapped up the grand slam.

By 1973 a new era was upon us. With the championships a week old, I noted that the survivors included 'three exciting youngsters in Bjorn Borg, 16, Martina Navratilova, 16, and Christine Evert, 18'. In the first round Borg beat Cliff Richey, seeded ninth:

'Richey, a pale-eyed, tough little Texan known as 'The Bull', is champion of South Africa and has long been a tenacious competitor on clay. Today he was astonished by a 16-year-old Swede called Borg, whose name has caused a buzz of excited speculation in world tennis for the past 12 months. Borg, of course, had nothing to lose except a tennis match. But the dynamically aggressive Swede treated Richey as if the Texan was little more than a hole in the air.'

Ilie Nastase won the men's singles without losing a set. But the women's final, featuring great players of different generations, was the bonne bouche. The first half of my report will serve our purpose:

'Margaret Court today became the only player except Suzanne Lenglen to win the French tennis championship five times. Mrs Court has a 16-month-old son. She will be 31 next month. Yet she survived a cruelly arduous physical and emotional ordeal in beating Christine Evert 6–7, 7–6, 6–4 in a final that lasted two hours and a quarter on the centre court of the Stade Roland Garros.

In 1970 Mrs Court emulated the late Maureen Connolly by achieving a grand slam of the Australian, French, Wimbledon and United States singles titles. Again she has surmounted the first two hurdles, including the toughest of the lot, the French. Since 1960 she has won 32 of the traditionally famous singles championships: 11 Australian, five French, four American and three Wimbledon, Italian, German and South African titles. We may never see her like again.

Mrs Court's astonishing competitive qualities, her refusal to accept defeat even when logic most firmly insists on it, have never been better demonstrated than they were today. She missed her chances in the first set, in which she won 11 of the first 12 points, led 4–1, had two set points at 6–5, and in the tie-break led 5–2 with two services to come. She looked done for when she played a loose service game to go 3–5 down in the second set. In retrospect, the next game was the key to the match. Miss Evert made two errors on each flank to lose the game to love.

Even so, it seemed unreasonable that Mrs Court, conceding 12 years and five months, should come back to win. Yet she won a thrilling tie-break game in which three successive shots (two of them Mrs Court's) hit the lines after Miss Evert had led by five points to four. Then Mrs Court came out for the third set, in which the odds favoured the younger player, and somehow found the reserves of strength and stamina to increase the pressure. She led 4–1. Miss Evert fought back to 3–4, then made three errors to go 3–5 down. There was a lot of excitement to come. But Mrs Court was the sounder in the last trembling crisis. The last two points were decided by backhands down the line. Mrs Court hit one in. Miss Evert hit one out.

Even then, when it was over, we could hardly believe that Mrs Court had come back from a set and 3–5 down to win. She has been (and remains) one of the greatest players in the game's history. No woman can challenge her impact on the records. Yet in our awed respect for this astonishing woman we can also admire the remarkable qualities of her precocious rival. Miss Evert reached the last four of her first two United States championships and did the same last year at her first Wimbledon. Here, again competing for the first time, she lost only 14 games in the five matches she played to reach the final: and then, amid the daunting immensity of the colourfully crowded centre court, produced her best tennis (at least, for much of the match) against a player whose very name must frighten any youngster conscious of what happened in all our yesterdays.'

In November of that year Miss Evert became engaged to Jimmy Connors and in 1974 she and Borg, two teenagers who did as much for the two-fisted backhand as Heinz did for beans, became champions of France. Connors and Evonne Goolagong, Australian champions, were among the players barred from Roland Garros in 1974 because they had competed in America's controversial new inter-city competition, World Team Tennis. The game's bungling administrators, who repeatedly get into a dither when confronted by independent commercial initiatives, decided that players and public must pay for the birth of WTT. Connors won a grass-court tournament at Manchester and then joined me on a flight to Paris. He wanted to spend a few days with his fiancée before resuming his preparation for Wimbledon.

We shared a taxi from the airport to Roland Garros, because I had to dive straight into a day's work, and the taxi then drove on the Jimmy's hotel. He had no French currency and borrowed 50 francs or so to pay the fare. Next day he paid me back. That trivial incident of the taxi fare had a sequel 11 weeks later, in New York, just before the United States championships. Gastro-enteritis had forced Connors to scratch from the final of a tournament in New Jersey and, having foolishly arranged to collect travellers' cheques on a bank holiday, I had arrived in Manhattan with about four dollars in my pocket. As we swopped bad news, Jimmy pulled out a roll of bills and asked me how much I needed. That was no big deal. He was a rich man. Then he added: 'You lent *me* money when I needed it. Remember?' Jimmy had not forgotten that taxi fare. I gave him a big plus mark.

In Paris, Connors did no more than put in a brief appearance as a spectator. Chris Evert and Borg both wore yellow for the 1974 finals. Borg became the youngest winner of the men's singles and there was further historic significance in an incident recorded in this 'intro' dated June 11:

'The startling advent of dope tests naturally overshadowed everything else that happened in the French tennis championships here today. Jan Kodes, twice champion, was beaten in straight sets last evening by François Jauffret, who is supposed to lose to Kodes in five sets rather than defeating him in three. Moreover, for two days Jauffret had been having treatment for some damaged fibres in his left thigh. Someone put the idea into Kodes' head that he should ask for a dope test, and this he did. Pierre Darmon, the tournament director, said that they might have refused the request but for the fact that a Frenchman was under suspicion. Both players provided urine samples and these were given to the analysts. The tests proved negative.'

The only man to beat Borg in the French championships was Adriano Panatta, who did it twice: in 1973, when Borg was an adolescent, and in 1976, when Borg was a man. Panatta, mind you, had nothing to lose after the 1976 first round:

'Adriano Panatta, who became champion of Italy three days ago, beat an ambidextrous Czechoslovak called Pavel Hutka in the French tennis championships here today. But if ever a bald fact demanded embellishment, that one does. The score was 2–6. 6–2, 6–2, 0–6, 12–10. In the fifth set Hutka had two break points for 5–3 and, having five times been poised within two points of victory, had a match point at 10–9. Panatta, four times, had to hold his service to save the match. Three times, he served to win it.

The rally that ensued on Hutka's match point deserved celebrating in poetry, painting, or music. Prose seems an inadequate medium. But it must serve our purpose. For a few moments the huge crowd in the sunny arena of the centre court murmurously savoured the drama to come. Then a hush descended on them— one of those eerie silences peculiar to vast assemblies. Panatta, his emerald green shirt darkened with sweat, perhaps said a private prayer as he arched his massive frame and dispatched his first service. Fault. Each man fidgeted a little. Around them, no one stirred. The silence had an awful tension in it. Second service, Then the fun began. Hutka's return clipped the net cord. Panatta, coming in, had to break his stride but hit deep and dominated the net—a swaying, apprehensive figure in green, like a tree trembling from one gust and awaiting the next.

Hutka lobbed. Briefly, it looked a winner. But Panatta, taxing to the limit the spring nature gave him, swung at the soaring ball and reached it with the frame of his racket. The shot that crossed the net was like something out of a tennis tea party. Hutka went for a cross-court backhand passing shot. There was, it seemed, lots of room. But on the other side of the net there suddenly appeared a reasonable approximation of a torpedo. It was Panatta, flinging himself headlong like a goalkeeper in the dying seconds of a World Cup final. He hit a winning backhand volley, then crashed onto the brick-coloured shale while the stadium thundered and echoed with the public's appreciation of a point that—isolated from the context of one game in one match—somehow captured the essence of the pleasure and pain, the beauty and drama, that is tennis at Roland Garros.

All that mattered after that was that Hutka, who had maintained his game at a remarkably high level for a remarkably long time, suddenly made three crucial errors—one tactical, two technical—while Panatta, puffing out his chest and looking proud and serious, flicked through a few pages of appendices with the cursory authority of a man who had read it all before (a week ago, he had 11 match points against him in the first round of the Italian championship).'

That was only the first half of my published report of the day's play. On no other occasion have I devoted 300 words to a single point. Except for sorting out the three 'thats' at the beginning of the last paragraph, I would not change a word of it. On the other hand I confess to slightly unprofessional conduct towards the end of the men's final. Panatta took two hours and 48 minutes to beat Harold Solomon, whose limpet-like pertinacity could drive opponents to headache pills and hints of delirium. The press are supposed to maintain a dispassionate decorum, but I kept dashing out of the telephone room to give Panatta a yell of encouragement over the last lap. My report was written. A deadline was imminent. And impatience had doubtless been lubricated by a glass or two of wine.

Solomon deserved sympathy. His bottle was almost empty, because he had played four five-set matches and the last of them, against Raul Ramirez the previous day, had taken three hours and 18 minutes. Ramirez elicited much in this vein:

'Ramirez is proudly straight-backed, yet expressive. At times he seems to impart a shrug to his eyebrows and his moustache. He spends a lot of time on his toes, in the springy way dancers have. Ramirez is fast when he needs to be, and quick-witted enough to fox most players who challenge his touch on volleyed drops and short angles. When going well, he plays to the gallery—savouring the moment by striking poses after striking winners.'

One evening in 1980 or 1981 David Irvine (*The Guardian*) was late in joining the rest of us for dinner and, when he did, almost choked on his steak. He was in a choleric mood. Frustration had been heaped upon frustration. There had been prolonged difficulty in making contact with a copy-taker. David's blood was simmering nicely when the Roland Garros operator connected him to London for the umpteenth time. At last, a copy-taker was available: and, as David admitted, he was a master of the craft. A smooth 'take' must have taken 15 minutes or so. Relieved, David went through to the sports desk to explain the delay—and discovered that *The Times* not only had my story, but his too. Wrong number. Wrong paper. We all have days like that, even at Roland Garros.

The 1982 men's singles final was an example of those occasions when a reporter must extemporize, or write against the clock, yet maintain a sense of perspective and tell the unvarnished truth about a historic occasion:

'Mats Wilander of Sweden, 17 years and nine months old, who was competing for the first time, won the French championship by beating Guillermo Vilas 1–6, 7–6, 6–0, 6–4 in four hours and 42 minutes here yesterday. The final was an admirably deplorable exercise in physical and mental stamina on a humid afternoon when the temperature was 27°C in the shade and 36°C in the open. It was also an embarrassingly boring example of the depths to which clay-court tennis can sink under the weight of careworn, top-spun driving from the baselines.

Above all, though, it was the last chapter in one of the most amazing stories in the history of tennis. Wilander became the youngest of French champions on the 26th birthday of the previous youngest champion, his compatriot Bjorn Borg, who has won the title six times—more often than anyone else—but did not defend it this year.

Wilander also became the only player except Ken Rosewall (1952 and 1953) to win the French junior and open championships in consecutive years. In his last four matches Wilander beat Ivan

Lendl, Vitas Gerulaitis, Jose-Luis Clerc and Vilas: respectively ranged third, ninth, sixth and fourth in the world.

Just think about all that. It is the stuff of schoolboy fiction, even fairytales. A curly-haired, genial lad from a town called Växjö, tucked away in a forest, suddenly jumped from obscurity to win the most gruelling tournament in the calendar. Within a week or so a boy became a man and a star was born (the clichés are irresistible).

Wilander's performance should be remembered for its romantic and historic connotations, rather than the fact that his ultimate success seemed to be chiselled out of stone. "I could not have beaten him any other way," Wilander said later.

The second rally contained 59 shots and set a pattern for the match. We began to wonder whether the best of five sets meant the best of five days. Those top-spun drives soared yards over the net and towards the end of the second set a rumble of thunder suggested displeasure in high places. The players' socks were soon encased in shale. The heat was awful, the gathering storm clouds merciful in their effects if not in their implications.'

And so on ... How pampered we were, in earlier years, by the mixture of subtle artistry and flashing sword-play spread before us by Pietrangeli, Santana, Laver, Rosewall, Emerson, Nastase and Panatta. But the breed had not died. By 1983 a revival was stirring. That year, too, the women had fun. Kathleen Horvath achieved an astounding win over Martina Navratilova and, as this extract shows, British reporters had something special to write home about:

'Joanna Durie of Bristol, aged 22, will play Mima Jausovec for a place in the women's singles final of the French championships. Yesterday Miss Durie gave what may have been the finest performance of her career. She beat Tracy Austin 6–1, 4–6, 6–0.

As the scores suggest, Miss Austin was completely outclassed in the first and third sets. Miss Durie playfully commented later, with a wink: "I lost the second because I needed the clay-court practice."

There is much in common between Miss Durie and the youngest player to win the women's title, Christine Truman. Miss Durie, too, raises images of schoolgirl heroines, observes the social proprieties, yet has an unaffected charm, a sense of fun, and a no-nonsense approach to life. In short, she is no goody-goody. Like Miss Truman, she is a six-footer who gives the ball a whack and has no great taste or talent for fancy stuff. Like Miss Truman, she is most obviously at home on fast courts but, oddly, has first reached the heights on the slow clay of mainland Europe.

Miss Truman used to say that she wished she could always play as she did when beating Sandra Reynolds 6–0, 6–0 in the 1959 Italian final. Miss Durie may come to have similar feelings about yesterday's match. It was no flash in the pan. She has reached the last 16 of the other three grand slam championships and, here in Paris, has beaten seeds in three consecutive matches.

Miss Durie has advanced fast since November, 1980, when she had an operation for a prolapsed disc in her back. For the last week she has been nursing a slightly strained groin muscle but has practised daily with Alan Jones, her coach, "to get warm, get moving, and get with it".

She certainly got with it yesterday. This was a bravura performance: exemplary in its mature authority, in its tactical variety, and in the timing with which Miss Durie used a wide range of shots. She was so boldly competent that she even played the clay-court tricks as if born to the trade: swinging the ball deeply to the corners to open up the court, or teasing Miss Austin with the quick one-two of a drop and passing shot.'

In the same round Chris Lloyd was playing Hana Mandlikova when a sideshow gave them an enforced breather:

'They had an enchanting match on an afternoon of bright,

sultry heat. Play was interrupted in the second set by an unin-
hibited fist fight between two spectators, one of whom finished it
off with a head butt at a time when he was losing on points. The
umpire had to remind the public to concentrate on the spectacle
on court, where Miss Mandlikova eventually yielded rather
despondently and was beaten 4–6, 6–3, 6–2.'

That was a relatively amusing example of the unpleasant scenes,
on and off court, that must be brought to the reader's attention
by any reporter who is doing his job properly. There are equally
rare days when, bursting with happy thoughts, one settles down
at the typewriter (preferably flanked by a glass of wine) in the sure
knowledge that the task ahead will be agreeable. Thus it was one
afternoon in June, 1983:

'José Higueras spent three hours and three-quarters playing the
champion, Mats Wilander, in roasting heat during the French
championships here yesterday. Wilander won 7–5, 6–7, 6–3, 6–0.
Then Higueras, still streaming with sweat (and trying to hide the
disappointment of defeat and the pain from an overworked
elbow), went to a press conference and answered a barrage of
questions with patient courtesy.

Eventually there was a pause and Higueras asked quietly: "May
I say something about Mats?" Of course. "It is a pleasure to play
against him", Higueras went on, carefully sorting out the words
he wanted in a language that was not his own. "He is a very good
tennis professional. We need players like him at the top, to help
the game". That was all. There was no need to gild the lily.

Higueras was maintaining the theme of a day's tennis that,
although it was anything but memorable in terms of excitement
or artistic content, opened windows in the mind. Could it be that
such concepts as "a sportsman and a gentleman" and "fair play"
are making a comeback in professional tennis?

Yannick Noah beat Christophe Roger-Vasselin 6–3, 6–0, 6–0 in the most embarrassingly one-sided semi-final since Bjorn Borg beat Vitas Gerulaitis in 1979. But there was a sympathetic rapport between them, first on court and then later, in the things each had to say about the other. Higueras and Wilander, diligent though they were in their attention to business, observed the sporting code as if it was the natural thing to do. And we may be sure that in the women's singles final Chris Lloyd and Mima Jausovec will not let the side down—another half-forgotten cliché that could now be restored to the tennis vocabulary.

The players concerned, mind you, are by no means softies. Wilander, with all the battle-hardened wisdom of a boy doing a man's job, firmly made the point that he came here to win the championship rather than entertain the public. The reminder was superfluous. He is more aggressive, more familiar with the forecourt, than Borg was at the same age. But the two Swedes play much the same way and are boring to watch (one still thinks of Borg in the present tense) because of their excessive dependence on top-spun drives from the baseline.

If Wilander, at the age of 18, finds it natural to step backwards—behind the baseline—after whacking a first service into court, how much fun is he going to get out of tennis or give to those who pay to watch him? Henri Leconte said recently that he would burn his rackets if he had to play like Wilander or another Swede, Joakim Nystrom. "To keep the ball in court while waiting for an opening is one thing. To wait for the other man to make a mistake is another. I would shoot myself rather than do that."

But wait. Yesterday produced another reminder that we may soon be dancing the old-fashioned way: Noah reached the men's final. He combines athleticism, power and touch better than any other finalist here since the prime of players like Rod Laver, Ilie Nastase and Adriano Panatta. What a marvellous match Noah should have with Wilander, who has been beaten only once in his last 50 singles on European clay. The man who beat him was Noah.

The details of yesterday's matches do not matter much. Roger-Vasselin was only a shadow of the player who beat Jimmy Connors (the Frenchman has since had hardly a moment to call his own) and was totally outclassed by Noah. Higueras, the more prone to take initiatives with a drop shot or an advance to the net, took two hours and 40 minutes to split sets with Wilander but had little more to offer. "It was very hot, I was doing a lot of running, I was a little tired, and my arm was very bad."

Britain's last contenders were beaten: Joanna Durie and Anne Hobbs in the women's doubles and John Lloyd—partnering Wendy Turnbull—in the mixed doubles. How pleasant it was to take time off from the rather humdrum singles to enjoy the better entertainment provided by the doubles. There was a time when doubles had a much more important role on the tennis stage than they have now. Perhaps that role will be restored to them. Yesterday certainly suggested that the good old days may soon be kicking up their heels again.'

Granted more time to think, I would probably have omitted Nastase from the trio of players who, like Noah, combined power with athleticism and touch. But fast-working reporters are not always punctilious. The final was close but Noah just managed to end it at a time when he was tiring and Wilander was improving. An extract will suffice:

'The men's singles champion of France is a Frenchman—for the first time since 1946. Yannick Noah, aged 23, subdued Mats Wilander, last year's winner, by 6–2, 7–5, 7–6 in two hours and 24 minutes here yesterday. We could only guess what was going on inside the inscrutable Wilander—a lad of 18 who was trying to resist not only Noah and most of the sell-out ctowd of 17,000, but also the will of a nation.

Wilander's game told us all we needed to know: he was far more erratic than he could afford to be. He could not keep enough rallies going, nor had he the attacking resources to finish enough of them in his own favour.

This was a triumph not only for Noah and France and Africa (while playing professional football in France, Noah's father married a Frenchwoman), but also for clay-court tennis. For almost a decade—what might be called the Borg era—this tournament has been dominated by baseliners specializing in top-spin. They were mostly two-fisted on the backhand and their aim was to wear down their opponents and induce indiscretions.

This was a joylessly negative way to play tennis. By contrast, Noah is a throwback to the days when good athletes with the spirit of adventure in them could win here: as long as they had sound ground strokes, a reasonably sure touch, and the sense to know when to attack. Tennis the Noah way is exciting.

Noah was born in France, brought up in Cameroun, which was formerly under French administration, but returned to France in 1973 after Arthur Ashe had spotted him during a goodwill tour of Africa. Noah sports a mop-headed, braided hair-style. What matters more is that there is 6 ft 4 in and almost 13 st of him, all of it arranged to produce maximum spring and strength and reach, plus a quivering energy that never seems to be totally in repose.

Noah is rather like Jimmy Connors in the Tarzan act he puts on when an important point has been won. At times there is a wild look about him, not least when he is pacing restlessly about the back of the court between points like a tiger impatient for dinner.

What extraordinary scenes there were when Wilander hit the last shot of the match, a wayward service return. The crowd had been simmering with excitement in bright, sultry heat, voicing thunderous roars of approval or collectively shushing themselves with a noise like the sea creeping up a shingle beach. At the end they boiled over—most spectacularly, Noah's father, who leapt from a high wall at one end of the court and fell on his bottom with a thud.'

The word dictated was probably 'bum' rather than 'bottom'. Some prim sub-editor may have decided I was overdoing the vernacular. You may have noticed that the reference to 'bright, sultry heat' has cropped up before. But how else would you describe bright, sultry heat? I once had a charming letter from a lady in Wisconsin who gently chided me for using the same analogy twice in three years. It had something to do with Roy Emerson taking us back to the time when a man had to catch and kill his dinner before eating it. I pleaded guilty but craved her indulgence. After three years, could I not be forgiven for taking the image down off the shelf and giving it another airing? The repetition of a trenchant quotation is even easier to justify. Anyone who can string a few words together should be able to write a passably interesting piece when players with big reputations get to grips on a big occasion. The test of a professional reporter is to produce a readable article on a day when nothing in particular is happening to nobody in particular. The second day of the 1984 championships was so relentlessly wet that we had only one result to consider. Catherine Tanvier beat Lucia Romanov: an event hardly calculated to drive one's readers in the Western Highlands (or anywhere else for that matter) into paroxysms of spluttering excitement. That result was noted in the course of a 600-word piece that blended the topical, the colourful, and the controversial. Abe Segal's comments about East Europeans, already noted on page 16, served as an introduction to this paragraph:

'Today's clay-court specialists, East Europeans included, are not all that different. They have the same strong legs and tired eyes, the same air of subdued suffering—as if aching somewhere or convinced that they soon will be. Many have seemingly fictional names and take part in seemingly endless but (usually) ultimately irrelevant matches. And around them are the massed ranks of the French—the only people, one suspects, who can shrug with their mouths.'

A few days later I had the pleasure of writing about Higueras again. Come to think of it, I would rather write about Higueras than watch him play tennis. He was beaten 6–4, 7–6, 3–6, 6–3 by John McEnroe. Three paragraphs summed up the occasion, the players, and the play:

'The day was grey and humid, the cloudscape dramatic. Twice, the players had to retreat to the dressing room while many spectators sheltered from the rain under that renowned horse chestnut on the promenade. But the sounds of the centre court, its musical score, were true to tradition—the rustle of shoes on shale, the muted thud of ball on racket, the drone of aircraft, and the tense silences—punctuated by scattered coughs—of the enraptured thousands. The crowd was not far short of the arena's 16,500 capacity.

The tennis was in the hands of two fine players who provided striking contrasts in personalities and playing methods. McEnroe, smouldering with ill-suppressed anger at his failure to achieve perfection, fretted about this and that but played some enchanting tennis—notable for his delicacy of touch on volleyed drops and his knack of suddenly accelerating the pace, often by taking the ball early.

Higueras is a dark and handsome Spaniard with an air of patient suffering. What a companion he would be on the mountains: he never hurries, never tires, never flinches in the face of adversity, and never does anything daft. Higueras is a fine sportsman, too. Once, he refused to take a point that did not belong to him. His tennis is assiduously homespun. An improvized splendour is sometimes forced upon him, but he never seeks it.'

Never tires? Not quite true. At the age of 31 even Higueras was looking around for a new engine. Another charming and careful man, Balazs Taroczy, popped up in my 'intro' next day:

'Balazs Taroczy is a mild-mannered man whose tennis reflects his capacity for deep thinking. When extraneous factors affect his professional labours, Taroczy's response is not that of a John McEnroe. He considers the problem quietly. Thus it was when lightning flashed around the French championships at a time when Taroczy and Yannick Noah had each won a set and were exploring the possibilities of a third.

Taroczy, in his thoughtful way, asked the umpire why they were still on court. After all, he said, the celestial electricity system was on the blink and they would be safer indoors. They were still out there, the umpire told him, because it was not raining. "But I don't want to die here", Taroczy said. Their joint exercise in a logic that flirted with philosophy was terminated by the second deluge of the day. Taroczy had his way.'

There follows an abridged version of a report which attracted so many compliments that I am almost embarrassed (not a prevalent affliction among journalists):

'The players seeded to contest the singles finals of the French championships will do so: Martina Navratilova v Chris Lloyd and John McEnroe v Ivan Lendl. The gods who look after such things spent yesterday preparing a feast rather than serving one. There were three good matches, but none will linger in the memory.

Miss Navratilova walked on the edge of darkness for a while before beating Hana Mandlikova 3-6, 6–2, 6–2. The best performance of the day, because its margin was unexpectedly clear-cut, was Lendl's 6–3, 6–3, 7–5 win over Mats Wilander. There were 18 service breaks. Jimmy Connors, who served for the first set at 5–4 but lost the next six games, was beaten 7–5, 6–1, 6–2 by McEnroe.

Most of this occurred on an afternoon when the centre court, packed to its 16,500 capacity, was a cauldron simmering in bright, burning heat. True, Miss Navratilova and Miss Mandlikova went to work on a grey morning. Lendl and Wilander seemed to play through a change of climate. Clocks and watches, which do not capture the essential nature of such matches, insisted that they slugged it out for only two hours and 46 minutes.

The match seemed longer because of the monotonous baseline exchanges. One joker started a rumour to the effect that, outside the stadium, bouncers were throwing people in. The promenades became busy because many spectators decided that, as nothing interesting was happening, they might as well stretch their legs or queue for refreshments.

One British photographer said he took all the pictures he needed while Lendl and Wilander were playing one rally. Without shame, I confess to escaping for half an hour to a leafy cabin in the Bois de Boulogne and lunching on pâté and coffee, with a dog's head on my lap and optimistic sparrows hopping across the table. They were better company than Lendl and Wilander.

Lendl, mind you, played the game he had to play—and played it well. Showing far more initiative than Wilander (which is not saying much), he rallied patiently but was always alert for a chance to get to the net and do something terminal—usually on the basis of a fierce service or forehand. The clash of wills was almost audible and the outcome was in doubt to the end.

For McEnroe, time often seemed to stand still, awaiting his bidding. That was because of the frictional shale surface, which takes the pace off the ball, and because of McEnroe's remarkable reactions and powers of anticipation. What a marvellous touch he had, too. But being the kind of chap he is, McEnroe stamped the match with an ugly form of beauty. He was fined more than £1,400 for abusing a linesman.

Miss Navratilova's muscular skills contrasted with the daring, graceful fragility of Miss Mandlikova's tennis. Miss Mandlikova had two chances to take charge, one in the second set and another in the third, but she could not tighten the screw—partly because of something inside her and partly because Miss Navratilova's nerves, often twanging, were under control when most it mattered.'

Our sports editor, Norman Fox, spotted that reference to my half-hour dereliction of duty. When we talked on the telephone that evening he teased me about an appropriate deduction from salary.

On the big occasion one is particularly eager to produce a carefully considered and well written report. But the 1984 men's final lasted so long that there was no time to consider and no time to write. The typewriter was untouched. When the match ended, a deadline was pressing and I was already on the telephone, with reporter and copy-taker poised for an extemporized piece. In retrospect, this did not put enough emphasis on McEnroe's increasing tiredness, the decline in his service, and the fact that a player of his class should not have let Lendl off the hook. Moreover, my report of the women's final had to be cut, by my colleagues in London, because I exceeded my allocation of space. It is difficult to be precise about length when extemporizing. For better or worse, this is a slightly abbreviated version of my off-the-cuff piece:

'Ivan Lendl beat John McEnroe 3–6, 2–6, 6–4, 7–5, 7–5 in four hours and seven minutes in yesterday's men's singles final at Roland Garros. It eventually became a great sporting contest, with almost every point chiselled out of stone. The result meant that McEnroe had been beaten for the first time this year, that Lendl had at last won a grand slam singles title after finishing runner-up four times, and that both the French singles champions were born in Czechoslovakia.

The men's final fell into three phases. During the first McEnroe served so well that in 10 service games he conceded only 10 points. He did everything with such confident authority, such dextrous precision, that Lendl began to look bemused. He seemed to have little idea which way he would have to go next. He could not anticipate McEnroe's intentions.

The second phase began midway through the second set when McEnroe, angered by distracting noises, grabbed the head-set from a television cameraman and yelled into it. McEnroe was getting edgy and the crowd became excited. Lendl, spotting a glimmer of hope, began to hit harder and run faster. He gradually came to a greater understanding of McEnroe's game, as if suddenly finding the way to finish a jigsaw puzzle.

In the fourth set McEnroe was twice a break up, but the scales were obviously quivering. McEnroe was looking weary and talking to himself. It seemed that Lendl might now be the stronger man. As for the passionate crowd, they were no longer mere spectators. They were at one with the players in grasping every ray of hope and feeling the shock of every frustration.

That second phase was rather patchy. But the fifth set raised the match to an intensely dramatic level. Each player had two break points. McEnroe went down full length for the second time in the match. Serving at 4–5, he came within two points of defeat. Serving again at 5–6, he finally had to yield. He put a forehand volley in the net, was beaten by two forehand passing shots, and then narrowly missed the mark with a forehand volley. Lendl's cross-court backhand passing shots were a prominent feature of the critical phases of a remarkable match. Neither player could take charge, but it seemed that neither would ever wilt.

Above all, the championships will be remembered for a unique feat. Martina Navratilova became the first player, man or woman, to achieve concurrent grand slams in singles and doubles. She and Pam Shriver became the first team to achieve a grand slam in women's doubles.

Miss Navratilova beat Chris Lloyd 6–3, 6–1 in the singles final. It lasted only 63 minutes and became one-sided when Miss Navratilova won six consecutive games at a cost of three points. She showed us a dazzling cornucopia of skills—the most beautiful demonstration of women's tennis I have seen in 25 years on the circuit. The diversity of expertise on view was breathtaking. It must be doubted if the players made more than a dozen unforced errors between them.'

One evening in 1985 I was sitting in an Auteuil restaurant, sipping a vin blanc cassis and browsing through *The Times*, when the patron set before me a sizzling cargo of snails. One of these promptly exploded into the air and landed at the other end of the table, spattering garlic juices over the tablecloth, the wallpaper, and me. The patron's propitiatory carafe of Beaujolais was roughly equivalent to the subsequent cost of dyeing my sweater to hide the stains. Next time I ordered crudités, which the patron delivered with an apologetic smile and: 'Ce soir, pas de bombe!' The tennis had its odd moments, too. Miss Navratilova gave a press conference while nursing her 4 lb 8 oz miniature Fox Terrier 'KD' (short for 'Killer Dog', she explained), which was disproportionately well equipped for sound reception. 'She's still trying to grow into her ears', said the champion.

Had there been an award for the best supporting actress that year, it would have gone to Gabriela Sabatini, aged 15, a dark-haired beauty from Buenos Aires. She was beaten 6–4, 6–1 by Mrs Lloyd in a semi-final but for 12 games looked born to play starring roles. After that she could hit and run no longer and therefore tried to shorten the rallies. She succeeded, but at her own expense. I referred to the way genuine champions, like Mrs Lloyd, can soak up punishment and then resiliently respond with their finest tennis:

'Mrs Lloyd certainly soaked up punishment. For almost an hour she resisted a rain of top-spun drives that buzzed around her ears. It is awfully tiring to reach up for such shots and return them with power and precision. And what wondrous variety there was in Miss Sabatini's backhand. She hit over it, she chipped it, she hit it down the line or cross-court. Her backhands were most spectacular when half-volleyed from the baseline with perfect timing. When such shots flew straight down the line, Mrs Lloyd stopped playing tennis. She just watched.

Miss Sabatini, moreover, is agile and already competent in the forecourt, with a natural assurance of touch on the volley and all

---

the right ideas about finesse. Her dextrous control of the racket head, in almost any situation, was that of a girl destined to play tennis ...'

Mrs Lloyd became the only woman to win the singles title six times:

'Mrs Lloyd took two hours and 52 minutes to beat Martina Navratilova 6–3, 6–7, 7–5 in what was probably the best women's final I have seen here in 25 years. It took the mind back to 1973, when Margaret Court beat Mrs Lloyd, then Miss Evert, by 6-7, 7–6, 6–4. In that final, too, Mrs Lloyd was playing a great athlete with intimidating physical advantages.

This physical edge has been most evident in the bounding agility and strength of wrist and forearm that has enabled Mrs Court and Miss Navratilova to hit returns of controlled power at times when most women would be reduced to lunging helplessness. On Saturday Mrs Lloyd's enduring quickness and fitness were no less remarkable than her unflinching will.

... Her last shot was breathtaking. Under pressure, she hit a fierce backhand down the line through a gap that could hardly have been narrower. "Chris played a great match", Miss Navratilova said. "She's playing better now than she ever has. It's nice to know that you can improve at 30!".'

Mats Wilander dined well on the pace Boris Becker fed him:

'The court became scarred and pock-marked as Wilander reminded the strong-armed German that playing shots is not the same thing as playing tennis. To put it another way, Becker played draughts while Wilander played chess—always thinking one or two moves ahead.'

Predictably, Henri Leconte's win over Yannick Noah was richly entertaining:

'These handsome, swaggering heroes—athletes, adventurers and actors, faithful to the tradition of Dumas and the Musketeers—had to play each other for a place in the last eight of the singles. Can you imagine a film in which Clint Eastwood and Sidney Poitier, both in their prime, were hunting the same villain?
... Leconte, left-handed, used to remind us of the young Rod Laver. But he was awfully wild. Now he is married and more mature. He plays one daft shot every two games instead of two daft shots every game. He can play like a dream, and has an unusual knack of shrugging with his mouth and eyebrows. Noah, who has the kind of build that inspires sculptors, is tense and twitchy and prone to punch the air—or bounce up and down like a boxer impatient to be let loose by his seconds.'

And so on. John McEnroe recovered from 1–3 down in the fifth set to win a thrilling match with Joakim Nystrom:

'The temperature hovered hazily between 102°F and 104°F and the match lasted three hours and 32 minutes ... The heat and humidity were awful ... The sweat that poured out of McEnroe and Nystrom would have filled a bucket ... Nystrom, who is 6 ft 2 in tall but weighs only 11 st wet through (which he was), seemed to become more spindly as the match progressed. It would have been no surprise to see steam rising from the congested terraces.'

The American challenge expired in the semi-finals. McEnroe and Jimmy Connors could not win a set between them. But McEnroe had a dazzling duel with Wilander:

'On the one hand was McEnroe's erratic, petulant brilliance; and on the other Wilander's unflinching composure and refusal to live beyond his means. Wilander never tried to match McEnroe's gift for improvised splendour ... At the heart of the match McEnroe was dream and nightmare in turn. Taking the ball early, he hit some backhands—mostly cross-court—that challenged belief. His swift anticipation and reactions, his deceptive timing and touch, his restlessly adventurous spirit, repeatedly transformed defence into attack. But his was a fragile beauty that did not impress Wilander, a nimble counter-puncher who was always at his best when clouds were gathering ... The prose writer was in better form than the poet.'

Wilander (a bolder, more versatile champion than the Wilander of 1982) was too good for Ivan Lendl in a final bedevilled by a gusty wind. The men's singles had again been a graveyard for the American dream. Since Tony Trabert was champion in 1954 and 1955, only five Americans—Herbie Flam, Harold Solomon, Brian Gottfried, Vitas Gerulaitis, and McEnroe— had reached the final. Only Solomon and McEnroe managed to win a set. Americans, men anyway, just don't seem to understand the language of Roland Garros.

A day at the French championships can mirror a lifetime's hope and frustration, beauty and pathos, pleasure and pain. In the past few years the emphasis has shifted slightly away from finesse. But that is probably no more than a passing phase ...

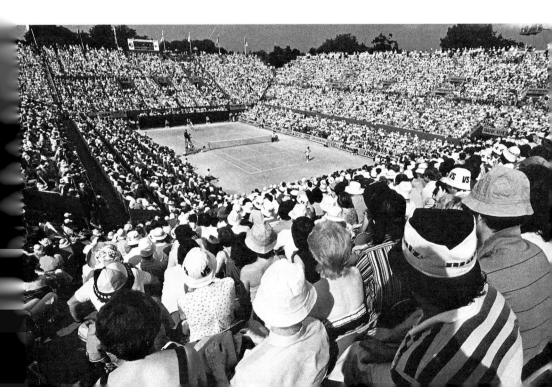

French tennis will long remember this sweltering Sunday afternoon.
At 4.20 the crowded centre court of the Stade Roland Garros – its four
banks ablaze with colour, like giant flower-beds – almost burst
asunder with noise and movement. France was saluting its first women's
singles champion since Nelly Landry (French by marriage) in 1948,
and its first French-born winner since Simone Mathieu in 1939 ...
    The new national heroine is Françoise Durr ...

Durr v Turner, 1967 Paris Final. 4–6, 6–3, 6–4

Miss Haydon beat the 18-year-old Miss Smith, twice Australian champion, by 7–5, 12–10 in an absorbing and increasingly tense test of mental and physical stamina that kept them on court for almost two hours of a sweltering afternoon . . .

Haydon v Smith 1961 Paris Final.

There was a great match today – played on a new 'show' court tucked away among the trees by a children's playground. Newcombe, already champion of the German and Italian clay courts, beat the 23-year-old Jan Kodes of Prague by 6–1, 6–4, 0–6, 8–10, 11–9 . . .

Newcombe v Kodes (above) 1969, Paris.

Paris is an annual reminder of the craft and culture lawn tennis can command and here was the world's finest hard court player, Santana, laying out his store of riches at the prompting of a perfect foil . . .

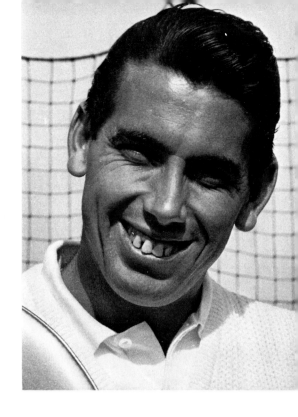

Santanta, 26, is at his peak. Pietrangeli, 30, is beyond it. He hardly ever trains and rarely goes to bed before one o'clock. If he went to bed early, he says, how would he occupy the mornings? Yet Paris always strikes a chord within him, for here the artist is king.

Santana v Pietrangeli (left), 1964 Paris final: 6–3, 6–1, 4–6, 7–5.

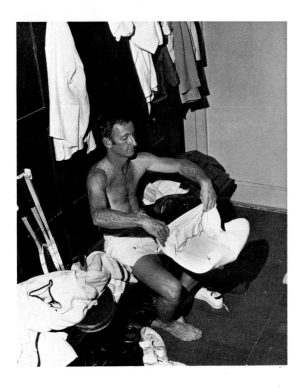

The introspective and awkwardly angular Laver looks a shy chap. He always seems in a hurry to get out of the public eye. He won yesterday because he has more experience of such electric storms as this match created – and is better equipped to survive them . . .

Laver v Ashe, 1969 Wimbledon semi-final. 2–6, 6–2, 9–7, 6–0.

Newcombe's is the kind of face that emerges victoriously through smoke and dust and a sudden flutter of flags at the end of those battle films. He kept baring his teeth, puffing out his chest, and looking fierce. To pass the time between Dibley's double-faults, Newcombe mopped his brow and rearranged his muscles.

Newcombe v Dibley, 1971 Wimbledon. 6–1, 6–2, 6–3.

Rosewall gave Tony Roche 10
years and beat him 10–8, 6–1, 4–6,
6–2. The 47 minute first set was
the finest of the championships.
Rosewall's performance overall
marked him as part magician, part
ordinary mortal, and all tennis
player ...

Rosewall v Roche, 1970
Wimbledon.

... here was a fine match between
two whippy, swift and restlessly
adventurous welterweights. Their
tennis was all timing, touch and
improvisation. Their shots
continually stepped with dainty
tread on the frontier between the
brave and the reckless ...

Laver v Okker (right), 1971
Wimbledon. 7–5, 6–1, 2–6, 7–5.

Hutka went for a cross-court backhand passing shot. There was, it seemed, lots of room. But on the other side of the net there suddenly appeared a reasonable approximation of a torpedo. It was Panatta, flinging himself headlong like a goalkeeper in the dying seconds of a World Cup Final. He hit a winning backhand volley, then crashed on to the brick-coloured shale while the stadium thundered and echoed with the public's appreciation . . .

Panatta (below) v Hutka, 1976 Paris. 2–6, 6–2, 6–2, 0–6, 12–10.

By contrast, Noah is a throwback to the days when good athletes
with the spirit of adventure in them could win here: as long as
they had sound ground strokes, a reasonably sure touch, and the
sense to know when to attack. Tennis the Noah way is exciting.

Noah v Wilander, 1983 Paris final. 6–2, 7–5, 7–6.

... Leconte, left-handed, used to remind us of the young Rod Laver. But he was awfully wild. Now he is married and more mature. He plays one daft shot every two games instead of two daft shots every game. He can play like a dream, and has an unusual knack of shrugging with his mouth and eyebrows ...

Leconte v Noah, 1985 Paris. 6–3, 6–4, 6–7, 4–6, 6–1.

Then Lendl saved a set point with a fierce forehand – and proceeded to blast McEnroe into submission with relentlessly powerful hitting. McEnroe hung on as best he could. But the pace and precision of Lendl's services, volleys and ground strokes never wavered.

Lendl v McEnroe, 1985 New York final, 7–6, 6–3, 6–4.

Ashe gave Connors speed of shot only when the need for variety –
or the chance of an outright winner – insisted on it. Even his service
was usually hit at three-quarter pace, in the interests of precision …
His length was superb. All was measured, calculated, unhurried.
During the changeovers Ashe relaxed utterly; so still that he might have
been in a trance. His self-discipline was total.

Ashe (right) v Connors, 1975 Wimbledon final, 6–1, 6–1, 5–7, 6–4.

Gonzales himself is one of the few personalities in Wimbledon's history who can dominate the centre court instead of allowing it to dominate him. The man smoulders with character ... Yet behind the animal is the artist, behind the lion a sporting surgeon with a wondrous delicacy of touch. This is a man who was born to greatness and did not scorn the gift.

Gonzales (41) v Pasarell (25), Wimbledon 1968, 22–24, 1–6, 16–14, 6–3, 11–9, 5 hrs 12 mins:

He opened the door and there you were in what had become your customary position of obeisance to the commode. Roy just picked you up and slung you over his right shoulder like a sack of wheat and carried you away. It was a memorable evening – one of our better parties. I'm sorry you missed it.

Bud Collins and Roy Emerson (above) v Rex Bellamy and The Commode, Boston 1967.

There is a tendency to assume
that tennis begins and ends at
Wimbledon, that no other event
matters much, that grass is the
best surface for tennis. Though
Wimbledon championships are the
most coveted in the game, the
assumptions are nonsense.

Wimbledon is a social occasion with a cosmopolitan guest list and a sporting raison d'être. On and off court, it is dominated by the manners and customs of the English middle classes. These respect the conventions of polite society and mostly vote Conservative.

CHAPTER TWO

Wimbledon: Smash and Grab

A PARADOX about the game's greatest festival is that it reduces tennis to a crude form—mere flashes of beauty, with no enduring flame. Rallies tend to be over before they become interesting. Much of the men's tennis at Wimbledon is drained of colour. Watching it is rather like travelling back in time to the era of black and white television. Another paradox is that the smash-and-grab raids of Wimbledon are un-British. The British are not renowned for the hasty violence that is the enemy of order, nor for the gambling instinct that challenges reason. But violent gambling is the nature of tennis as it is played on grass. One does not want standardized playing surfaces and their inevitable consequence, standardized playing methods. It just happens that an accident of history lumbered Wimbledon with grass—pretty to look at but, in terms of tennis as public entertainment, not even second best.

If Major W. M. E. ('Mike') White had not been such a good cricketer my introduction to Wimbledon would not be so deeply etched in the memory. In 1948 I was in the Army, doing the then obligatory stint of national service, and had a clerical job at Sandhurst. I spent a lot of time playing cricket, football, and table tennis and also worked on my mile time by dashing around the Royal Military Academy track with reluctant 'pacers' who had been talked into running alternate laps. It was at the RMA, too, that I first played squash. An oddity about the cricket was that I captained our college's staff team, which included officers, other ranks, and civilian tutors and therefore presented an unusual exercise in propriety when adjusting field placings: 'Captain Hamilton, would you move to gully? Harry, mid-off. Professor Hare, fine leg please'.

Mike White was our commanding officer and we often talked cricket. Unless memory lies, he was an off-spinner and had an attractive Yugoslav wife. One day he told me he had been invited to play for Northamptonshire and consequently could not escort his room-mate to Wimbledon. Would I deputize? Thus it was that I went to Wimbledon with the CO's wife and a few chums. Louise Brough and Bob Falkenburg won the singles that year but I can't remember a thing about the tennis—much less, any ambition to write about it. By 1979, 31 years on, I knew enough to describe the championships to American readers. The following piece, now slightly amended, was written for the magazine *World Tennis*:

'Wimbledon is a social occasion with a cosmopolitan guest list and a sporting raison d'être. On and off court, it is dominated by the manners and customs of the English middle classes. These respect the conventions of polite society and mostly vote Conservative. They tend to be slightly irritated if deprived of coffee at 11.0 ("elevenses") and afternoon tea at 4.0. It is not surprising that Wimbledon is as formal, as ritualistic, as a church service. Wimbledon, indeed, is the mother church of tennis. As we pass through the gates into the grounds there is a thrill of expectation, a faint twanging of the nerves, an awareness that we have arrived at a great occasion.

Everyone who takes part is conscious of the need to behave with propriety, to do "the decent thing", to avoid causing offence to others. Perhaps the chief influence in all this is the patronage by royalty. It is the accepted thing that players walking onto the centre court bow or curtsy towards any member of the royal family who happens to be present. The formality extends to clothing. Members of the All England Club, their distinguished guests, and even large segments of the public and the press corps tend to dress as they would for a social gathering rather than a day's sport. As a small private protest against the inhibiting primness of Wimbledon, I never wear a tie there. But the weight of traditional conventions is impossible to ignore and difficult to resist. Wimbledon is a bastion of conservatism.

There are ghosts at Wimbledon. They are friendly but rather intimidating—almost tangible in the enduring strength of their personalities. The greatness of yesterday can be sensed everywhere. The place is like an old house in which new owners are always conscious of those who lived there before them. The ghosts have names like Suzanne Lenglen, Bill Tilden, Henri Cochet, Helen Wills, Maureen Connolly, and Rod Laver. The players of today cannot close their minds to the players of yesterday. This is particularly true on the centre court. The stadium is both intimate and intimidating. Its perimeter is roofed, which gives the centre court an enclosed, concentrated, almost claustrophobic ambiance. There are times when the centre court has the character of an indoor arena. Its walled-in nature contrasts sharply with the openness of Roland Garros or Flushing Meadow or the Foro Italico. Many great players, men and women of strong personalities, have sometimes been overwhelmed by this powerful aura. For a few games they can be afflicted by a form of mental paralysis, so that they just hit balls instead of playing tennis. Only a few players— Lenglen, Tilden, Jean Borotra, Pancho Gonzales, Ilie Nastase among them—have dominated the centre court instead of being dominated by it.

Because of the sometimes irritating middle-class formality, the huge weight of tradition, and the special nature of the centre court, playing tennis at Wimbledon can be rather like holding a party in a churchyard. There can be no relaxed enjoyment of casual pleasures. Wimbledon is less fun than any other major tournament. But it does have many special and alluring features. There is, for a start, the green prettiness of the grounds. These are at their loveliest when figures in white are dashing about the courts on a sunny afternoon and the terraces and promenades are animated by a swarming crowd of 30,000 or more. The mighty walls of the All England Club are covered by creeper. So is the prominent water tower that looms over the outside courts. A church spire peeps over a wooded hillside. All that is typical of the charm of southern England—green, restful, a place for flowers and hedgerows and trees and birdsong. In short, the setting is part of the Englishness of Wimbledon.

The crowds mostly consist of knowledgeable tennis enthusiasts, plus a large section who go to Wimbledon simply because it is the thing to do. For the public (and indeed for the entire tennis community) Wimbledon is a rendezvous for a "family" reunion. The best time to appreciate this, while wandering at random around the outside courts, is during the first two or three days. After that the crowds often become unpleasantly congested. And during the second week the main matches are concentrated on the centre court and court one and the championships acquire a different, less pleasurable character. During the second week, the laughter drains out of Wimbledon.

The organization of the tournament is renowned for its slick efficiency. This is the result of years of practice, months of preparation, and the daily labours of an army of workers. There is painstaking attention to detail. Nothing is overlooked. The entire organization ticks over like clockwork. There is a smartly drilled, military precision about the administration. The All England Club appointed their first salaried secretary in 1907 and the first four holders of that post (until Christopher Gorringe took over in 1979) were all former officers in one or other of the Armed Services. The most successful tournament in the world is not the place for revolutionary changes. But the championships committee are making adjustments to meet the needs of modern tennis, while carefully preserving Wimbledon's unique qualities.

Wimbledon is given world-wide publicity by a cosmopolitan corps of men and women from all branches of the media. In

Britain itself, the impact of the publicity is inescapable, the public interest enormous. The direct television coverage is continuous, every day, and in the evenings there is an edited recording of the day's most interesting phases. The publicity is so comprehensive, so detailed, that everyone from Land's End to John o' Groats knows what is happening at Wimbledon and can hardly avoid being swept along by the flood tide of enthusiasm. They may not be particularly interested in tennis. But they are absorbed by the character of Wimbledon and the men and women who play there.

There is a tendency to assume that tennis begins and ends at Wimbledon, that no other event matters much, that grass is the best surface for tennis. Though Wimbledon championships are the most coveted in the game, the assumptions are nonsense. The game's most famous and most successful festival is played on an unusual surface. Grass courts are uncommon in the rest of the world. Most players are unfamiliar with them. They do not produce the most attractive tennis. It is true that the speed of grass-court tennis makes the women's game more spectacular than it is, for example, on clay. But men's tennis explores wider, more fascinating possibilities when played on slower surfaces. British enthusiasts, conditioned to believe that Wimbledon is the apogee of tennis in every way, tend to be startled and delighted when first confronted by the richer texture of the game played in such places as Paris and Rome.

The truth is that the nature of the tennis is among Wimbledon's least attractive features. The quality, the standard of play, is usually exemplary. But grass strips tennis to its fundamentals. There is not much profit in the graces of subtlety and finesse. There is not much time for patterned manoeuvring. Even Manuel Santana, so imaginative and artistic on clay, had to acquire a big service and carefully restrict his repertoire of shots in order to win Wimbledon. In other words, when winning Wimbledon he was less interesting, less fun to watch, then he was when winning in

Paris. On grass, the bounces are fast and usually low. The important things are power, fast reactions, a capacity for improvization. These qualities are necessary on any surface. But they are not enough, in themselves, to satisfy the connoisseur.

To sum up, we may say that the special features of Wimbledon are middle-class conventions, traditions, green beauty, huge crowds, superb organization, widespread publicity, and the unusual nature of tennis played on grass. The championships are impressive and their ambiance is thrilling, inimitable, and in many ways charming. Fun? Well, hardly that.'

Since that piece was written, Wimbledon has been enlarged and improved by the introduction of four new courts and the adjacent development of Aorangi Park—with its 'food village', restaurant, picnic area, souvenir shop, and demonstrations of 'short' tennis. The public now have more scope for relaxed, casual pleasures only indirectly connected with tennis-watching. The place has become less staid, though it still provides an exemplary study in the stratification of English society.

During the decade from 1975 to 1984 every national daily except *The Times* had a change of tennis correspondent—though John Parsons, who took over the *Daily Telegraph* job in 1981, had previously been tennis man at the *Daily Mail* from 1969 to 1971. Most of us learned the trade as 'leg men' and dogsbodies for older, more experienced predecessors. For seven or eight years I helped Geoffrey Green, a charming eccentric who cloaked his professionalism in a colourful mantle of dilettantism. Geoffrey was an artist, a romantic, who disciplined himself to excel in a craftsman's profession. His command of vivid imagery was remarkable and the riches of the English language spilled out of him so freely that he could not always channel the flow. Luckily for me this master of the ad lib was primarily 'Our Association Football Correspondent', as the by-line of those days put it, and in the early 1960s the soccer and tennis seasons increasingly overlapped.

Eventually Geoffrey found it difficult to fit in much more than Wimbledon and a few Davis Cup ties. In 1967 *The Times* resolved a slightly absurd situation by leaving him free to concentrate on his first love, soccer, and giving me the tennis job. The transition was well timed. That was the last year of shamateur competition. A new era was at hand.

Wimbledon often produces lovely tennis, in spite of the grass, and in 1967 there was a good example featuring Wilhelm Bungert, who was to reach the final (the next German to do that was Boris Becker in 1985). Here is an abridged version of my report:

'With five days gone, the persistently eventful Wimbledon championships are still maintaining the astonishing average of one seed beaten every day. Yesterday's victim was the French champion, Françoise Durr. But this was no more surprising than the defeat of a girl who should have been seeded: Kerry Melville.

There was, too, a classic match on the centre court between Wilhelm Bungert and Bobby Wilson, who delighted us for two hours and 25 minutes before Bungert finally subdued a man who himself had been within two points of winning.

As if all this were not enchantment enough, the setting was perfect—a gem of a day casting a lustre on the actors who trod the various stages and the bulging crowds who flocked to watch them. Here was a day bright with colour, drowsy with warmth, yet tingling with excitement—a Wimbledon, in fact, in all its glory.

To assess the Bungert–Wilson match in statistical terms would be like ordering porridge as an hors d'oeuvre when dining out in Paris ... The match was engrossing in its form, in the quickly shifting patterns of light and shade that fell first across one man, then the other. But what left such a delicious, lingering flavour on the palate was the style and grace, the flair and feeling, the wrist and reflexes, with which Bungert and Wilson took hold of a sport and turned it into an art form.

The second game—the first was formal—began a sequence of gorgeous rallies, flickering with the shining bladework of two fencing masters happy at their work. The first set was one of the finest Wilson has ever played. The second was another—after a swirling swarm of bees, sniffing something tasty, had descended on the court, interrupting play and causing a flutter in the crowd.

In prosaic terms, Bungert served 10 double-faults in those first two sets—but later served with blinding accuracy when it mattered even more. His chief weapon, as always, was that whipped forehand, a stroke which at times seemed to exist outside the world of human error.

Wilson sensibly aimed for the backhand—and won some big points there. But Bungert, a strolling player with a casual air, also has long legs, long arms, an enviable ability to read the rallies, and a wrist of steel with which to improvise his ripostes. He is a difficult man to corner.

Wilson's own touch and reflexes were often extraordinary. Time and again his remarkable wrist contrived a good return when the ball had already passed him. But after playing two sets in the clouds he was gradually brought down to earth and towards the end his first service—and his service returns—began to let him down. Yet he did not deserve to lose. The coming days can provide no finer exhibition of tennis than he and Bungert gave us yesterday.

The other men's matches were as water to wine.'

To fill in the obvious gaps, Bungert won 1–6, 5–7, 6–1, 7–5, 9–7; Miss Durr was beaten by Jan O'Neill; and I wrote of 'the disciplined yet rampaging violence of Virginia Wade's eventually crushing win over Miss Melville'. Four days later I was to lead my report with news of a match I had not seen—because it was played in the evening, when reporters are writing rather than watching. A new British partnership, Peter Curtis and Graham

Stilwell, reached the doubles semi-finals with a five-set win over the top seeds, John Newcombe and Tony Roche.

You will have noted that in 1967 I was still confused about the distinction between reflexes and reactions. But in those days at least there was time to sit down and write a considered, expansive piece for the later editions. The first edition report was a nerve-racking trip through a mental mangle. Play did not begin until two o'clock and, after a few hours chasing news like a squirrel collecting nuts, one had to extemporize 1,000 words straight out of the notebook—with nothing in sentence form. This used to drive me barmy. I wanted to do a good piece, incorporating a few fancy phrases, but knew the odds were against me. That first edition challenge was exciting, though. Equipped with a pint of beer, I would get on the telephone and hope for a patient but quick and competent copy-taker (in this respect *The Times* was, and is, well blessed) who would get me through the 1,000 words before the beer got through me.

The trouble with an ad lib is that one has no time to check or revise. One's syntax may be sloppy. An important fact may be overlooked. I solved this last problem by taking two-tone notes. At the end of every set I underline in red the rallies and comments that most matter. This avoids some of the hazards of extemporizing and is equally useful, of course, when settling down to write a piece. *The Times* and the times have changed. Nowadays there is seldom any need to ad lib at such length. Wimbledon starts earlier and my first edition reports are hurriedly typed between 5.30 and 6.45. Later, one merely does an 'add' or a 'rejig' (shifting or cutting a paragraph so that new material can be incorporated). The only other difference is that I drink wine instead of beer.

That reference to 'expansive' pieces became even more pertinent in 1968, when I often babbled on for 1,200 words or more. There was room to get into a match and explore its detail and character, without ignoring the rest of the day's doings. This, for example, was little more than half of one day's report:

'The first open Wimbledon yesterday produced its first great match when Ken Rosewall beat Charles Pararell by 7–9, 6–1, 6–8, 6–2, 6–3 on the centre court. They played for two hours and 26 minutes but three rain-breaks carried the match over a total span of three hours and 54 minutes.

It seemed an interminable delight and we wished that it could be. Come grey skies come blue, come rain come sunshine, come tea come martinis, Rosewall was always playing Pasarell—and it was getting better all the time. Here was a tennis match that will give a corner of the memory a sheen of gold.

Among the men who climb to high places there is a saying that the mountains bring you three things—men, battle, and beauty. The men are true, the battle is the only kind worth fighting, and the beauty is life. Rosewall and Pasarell took us to the mountains yesterday—and the air was like wine.

For two sets it was a good match. In the third the purple of greatness fell upon it and stayed there. It had all the necessary components—its content was of the highest class, its shape ach-ieved a dramatic crescendo, and its protagonists offered a perfect contrast in style and personality.

The interruptions probably helped Pasarell to maintain the velocity of his service. They probably helped Rosewall (what a wonderful scrambler he is!) to keep those little legs twinkling to and fro on arduous errands. They probably ensured, for all of us, a climax fit for the theatre.

The actors came from different schools. Rosewall is a quick and quiet man, so cool, so calculating, that even his strides between rallies seem to be measured to an inch. Pasarell, splay-footed, repeatedly hitching up his trousers, walks along the baseline as if strolling up to a bar and looking for trouble in an old-time Western.

Pasarell is a gambler, too. He gambled yesterday—on his explo-sive services and his full-blooded ground strokes. He gambled and he often won. The match caught fire at one set all. In the third

Pasarell led 4–0 and had a set point at 5–4. Rosewall saved it with an angled forehand so lovely, so unexpected, that it caught the breath.

Twice that set was interrupted by rain—the second time when Rosewall had served one fault at love–40 down and 6-all ("It was as good a time as any to pack up", said Rosewall later). The rules allowed him two balls when play was resumed almost an hour later. But Pasarell won that important game on his fourth break point.

At two sets to one up, Private Pasarell of the United States Army's Air Defence Command was justifying his leave of absence. But "The Little Master" was the duty officer in the next set. Here again there was an interruption, succeeded by sunlight—and a drama so rich in tension that actors and audience were suddenly at one. It was almost seven o'clock and Wimbledon was booming with the collective heart cries of the centre court.

Rosewall caught his man at two sets all. In the fifth Pasarell broke service first, lost the advantage, but had two points for a further break. Yet it was Rosewall who landed the decisive blow: in the eighth game he boxed beautifully to make his opening— and seized it by punching home a high backhand volley.

That left Rosewall serving for the match. But there was still some gorgeous tennis to come—and two break points to Pasarell. Rosewall fought him off. But when Pasarell put a last backhand out of court we could not believe that such a match was over. Nor is it: we shall tell our grandchildren about it.'

At the end of that day's report, having discussed a variety of other matches, I reverted to the same theme for my pay-off lines: 'Yet the abiding memory will be of Rosewall and Pasarell. If they show films in Valhalla, this is a match the gods will want to see.' A year later Pasarell again lost an epic match: and this one made history. The first day of the 1969 Wimbledon was washed out. At the end of the second day my piece began thus:

'Wimbledon's opening day was 24 hours late. But it was worth waiting for. Its high-speed expertise was punctuated by drama, contained the downfall of two seeds, and ended with a third, Ricardo Gonzales, booed off the centre court in the twilight, his match with Charles Pasarell suspended after Pasarell had won the first two sets.

The score at the time was 24–22, 6–1. The first set equalled the record set in 1962 by Nicola Pietrangeli and Nikola Pilic. From 4–5 down Gonzales successfully served 18 times to save the set, but lost his service at the 19th attempt after saving a total of 11 set points. He was finally beaten by a lob that dropped on the line after he had missed his smash.

Gonzales, 41, inimitably combined power with touch in his effort to resist the relentless pounding of the 25-year-old Pasarell. It was an uphill struggle all the way for the only grandfather in big tennis; and he became increasingly annoyed by the worsening light. By the time he was 1–4 down in the second set he was bursting with rage.

He shouted with anger and whirled his racket about as if desperately fighting off an adversary he could not see. At the end of that fifth game came one of the most extraordinary scenes in Wimbledon's history. Gonzales threw his racket at the umpire's chair, then kicked it towards the canvas. A noisy section of the crowd erupted in sympathetic response. "Stop play!" they shouted. "Off! Off!" Then came a slow handclap.

But play continued—with Gonzales like a wounded, tormented lion who had lost his way in some sepulchral jungle. He lost the set. Pasarell took swift evasive action as Gonzales again flung his racket at the chair. Gonzales stormed angrily from the court. The crowd booed him. They cheered Pasarell. It was deplorable that such explosive tennis should be played in such poor light; but it was equally deplorable that Gonzales should behave so badly.'

Yes, the old man was cross—and two sets down. But 24 hours later there was another story to write:

'Ricardo Alonzo Gonzales, the United States tennis champion of 1948 and 1949, now a silver-haired grandfather, yesterday won the longest and one of the finest matches in Wimbledon's history. He beat Charles Pasarell, a 25-year-old American Davis Cup player, by 22–24, 1–6, 16–14, 6–3, 11–9 in five hours and 12 minutes.

These 112 games surpassed the 93-game record set by Jaroslav Drobny and Budge Patty at Wimbledon in 1953. There have been longer matches elsewhere—but none in which a man of 41 has endured so well for so long. Gonzales lost the first two sets. In the fifth he was twice love–40 down on his own service. He survived a total of seven match points. Yet he won the last two games to love. His was one of the greatest individual achievements in tennis or any other sport.

On Tuesday night Gonzales was booed from the court because of his angry reaction to worsening light. He had lost the first two sets in two hours and 18 minutes. Yesterday he earned a tumultuous ovation after winning the next three in two hours and 54 minutes. Yet here was a man who could look back 20 years to a similar match—in which he lost the first two sets before beating Ted Schroeder in the United States final.

At the end there was inevitably sympathy for Pasarell, who beat the reigning champion, Manuel Santana, in the first round of the 1967 championships, lost to Ken Rosewall in a great five-set match in the second round a year ago, and was now on the losing end of yet another remarkable first round match.

If you are looking for some fun in the early rounds at Wimbledon, look for Pasarell. He is worth looking at, too. Splay-footed and broad-shouldered, he has the shambling gait of some Western heroes. He walks with a drawl, arms swinging menacingly at his sides as if itching for a challenge to a fast draw. But during the rallies he was all strength and aggression. He pounded away at Gonzales with relentless power. Gonzales bent before the assault. But he never broke.

Gonzales himself is one of the few personalities in Wimbledon's history who can dominate the centre court instead of allowing it to dominate him. The man smoulders with character. There are dark, brooding depths in his intense concentration. He has the loose-limbed ease of the natural athlete. He has the mannerisms of a well rehearsed actor treading a familiar stage—the fingers of his left hand flicking away the sweat and hitching his sodden shirt back onto his shoulders.

Yet behind the animal is the artist, behind the lion a sporting surgeon with a wondrous delicacy of touch. This is a man who was born to greatness and did not scorn the gift.

What enabled Gonzales to keep going, in addition to his physique and his courage, was his economy of effort—his facile blend of power and subtlety. What enabled him to win was his superb ability to play the big points well; sometimes by blasting through Pasarell's defences, sometimes by outflanking them with breathtakingly dangerous strokes in which the ball was not so much hit as caressed.

Five times in the fifth set Gonzales served to save the match. In three of those games he had match points against him. If ever the writing was on the wall, it was then. But, as often happens in tennis, the pressure finally swung from one man to the other— and when Gonzales is applying pressure in a crisis it is like watching a panther pouncing on his first good lunch for a month. One match point was enough.'

Note that Pasarell played 112 games but was a first round loser, and that *The Times* (then pernickety about nicknames) may have been the only newspaper in the world to insist on 'Ricardo' instead of 'Pancho'. In those days, too, the players—unlike today's pampered heroes—had no chairs to sit on during changeovers. Gonzales and Pasarell stayed on their feet for the longest match in Wimbledon's history.

That may have been the year when one of our photographers, Bill Warhurst, burst into the press room. He was starry-eyed.

'I've just seen a real woman out there—she's actually built like a woman!'

I scanned the order of play.

'Court 12?'

'That's right. How did you guess?'

'Easy. Kerry Harris. And she's every bit as nice as she looks.'

Kerry was one of these sensible and jolly Australians, of both sexes, who keep the circuit down to earth—but laughing. One is often asked if tennis reporters have favourites. Of course we do— favourite players and favourite people (occasionally identical). It does not affect a genuine professional's reporting. The bleak, cold metal of a typewriter is infectiously dispassionate. But one's choice of matches may be affected, simply because some players are better company than others. It may be the way they play or the kind of people they are. Sometimes personal preferences and professional priorities coincide, which is to say that somebody special plays a match that demands reporting at length. That is gratifying. On rare occasions one's gut reaction is at odds with patriotism and the prospect of a good 'British' story. People matter more than their origins.

That 1969 Wimbledon included a memorable semi-final in which Rod Laver beat Arthur Ashe 2–6, 6–2, 9–7, 6–0:

'The Laver–Ashe match was curious and furious. Three sets were one-sided. Only in the third was there any lasting semblance of equality. Much of the match was disputed at such a cracking pace, with each man playing off the other's speed of shot, that they seemed to be firing machine guns rather than hitting tennis balls. If you happen to like that sort of thing—and it was certainly breathtaking to watch—this was as fine an example as you could get of tennis expertise on a fast grass-court.

To any rational human being, controlling a tennis ball at this speed seems impossible. Hitting a ball hard is one thing. But hitting it so hard, so accurately, so often is another. This was all thunder and lightning. There were no half-measures. Each used attack as a means of defence. "The greatest peril coincides with the greatest hope." Albert Camus wrote that. Laver and Ashe must have read it. The quickness of their reflexes alone was astonishing. Each seemed to regard the other's blazing thrusts as a challenge, as if to say: "First man to baby a shot is a sissy."

The introspective and awkwardly angular Laver looks a shy chap. He always seems in a hurry to get out of the public eye. He won yesterday because he has more experience of such electric storms as this match created—and is better equipped to survive them.

The broad-shouldered, bony and bespectacled Ashe could match Laver's speed of shot. But he could not match Laver's speed of foot. Nor, after the first set, could he read Laver's game as well as Laver could read his. Laver was so fast that he hit winners when he was apparently beaten; and so versatile that Ashe could never be sure what was going to hit him next. Laver used every inch of the court. Both were particularly severe on the backhand.

"In the first set," said Laver, "he was hitting winners at will. I got embarrassed at one stage. I was picking up balls at the back of the court, ready to serve, knowing that he would hit another winner back." But in the second set Ashe scored only two points against service. In the third Ashe twice broke back. But Laver took his service again for the set at 9–7. The fourth set lasted only 14 minutes and Ashe scored only eight points. He hardly had time to adjust his glasses.'

The British heroine was Ann Jones, who beat Margaret Court in a semi-final and Billie Jean King in the final. This was red meat for the domestic publicity media. Our sports editor in those days was John Hennessy and after the final I met him in the press room. His excitement was perceptible. He had just called the office, he said. In addition to the match report they wanted a page one piece plus a Jones feature for the 'op-ed' page (opposite the editorial leading articles). There was not much time. How was I going to do it?

'I'm going to get two beers, light a pipe, plant the seat of my pants on that chair, and keep typing until I've finished.'

'Can I help?'

'Yes. You can get the beers, plus whatever you fancy. Then come back in an hour and start shifting the copy.'

And, bless his heart, he did. As editorial conferences go, my contribution was deficient in social graces. But there are times for cutting the cackle and getting on with the job. It is always exhilarating to be under pressure—assuming that one is confident, competent, and has done the necessary homework. Wimbledon is the tennis reporter's toughest challenge, because so much information has to be gathered so quickly from so many courts: and reported to a set length by a set time. That means writing against the clock while the evening's play is still in progress. The reporter puts the ball in play by typing his piece and dictating it to a copy-taker. The rest is up to sub-editors, computer operators, a variety of other experts in technology, and finally van drivers, British Rail, and newsagents.

The most brilliant articles are garbage unless they reach the office on time. That is the reporter's responsibility. Wimbledon is the only tournament at which one has the help of a dictator—that is, someone to shift the story by telephone in short 'takes' while the writer is pounding out the next 'take'. In this respect I got lucky. In the late 1960s Barry Newcombe (then *Evening Standard*, now *Sunday Express*), John Oakley (then *Evening News*, now *Press Association*), and Rex Bellamy became a threesome at work and play—that is, the dining table, notably in Rome and Paris. Barry began to help out at Wimbledon, making sure that my copy hit the deadlines, keeping an eye open for infelicities of content, and sometimes checking a fact. As reporters from evening and morning papers we came under stress at different times of day and were not competing for readers. In helping *The Times* when his own job was done, Barry had a long day. But that applies to every Wimbledon reporter. Moreover, he had to consider what he was going to write for the *Standard*'s early editions next morning, so it was useful to know what line the 'mornings' were taking.

The writer's Wimbledon begins with a preview or 'prelim' and ends with a 'wrap-up'. My 1970 preview indulged in some reflective asides about the game and its players:

'We should remember with gratitude the fact that Wimbledon, like a few other important championships, is what the United Nations is all about. Tennis players have the same human weaknesses as the rest of us. They hail from a diversity of political, racial, religious, and social backgrounds. But they work and live together the year round. Every day they face crises of a kind. They set us an example in that, through all the pressures, such old-fashioned virtues as tolerance and good humour survive.

So, too, does that precious flower, character. Take time off, at Wimbledon, to savour the people behind the players. Bob Lutz has the same forelock, the same air of puzzled resignation, as Dustin Hoffman in *The Graduate*. The lank-haired Zeljko Franulovic is as sleepily relaxed as Arthur Ashe and has the same habit, hand on hip between rallies, as another Dalmatian, Nikola Pilic.

Note the Rumanians, with Petre Marmureanu a sort of straight man to the knockabout comedy team of the gay, fiery Ilie Nastase and that hairy giant, Ion Tiriac, a Heathcliff of the courts. The tall and teethy Dick Crealy has a cockerel's walk, jerking his head forward.

Enjoy those bouncy little players, Rosemary Casals and Joaquin Loyo-Mayo, who both seem to be built on springs. Notice the contrast between the leading Czechoslovaks: Jan Kodes, a tight-lipped, hard-eyed introvert, and Alena Palmeova, bright-eyed and bursting with gaiety. If you have a thing about backhands down the line, watch the new Hungarian champion, Szabolcs Baranyi, or that 5 ft 11 in of elegant languor, Helga Niessen, who between rallies, takes up a cross-legged stance as if arrested in the middle of a pas de deux.

If you like fiery flyweights, watch the scampering, chatty Monica Giorgi. A lovely smile? Pat Walkden, Elizabeth Ernest, Lany Kaligis, or Kazuko Sawamatsu. Frilly glamour? Lea Pericoli or Maria Nasuelli. A touch of heterodoxy? Marijke Schaar or Lita Liem, both ambidextrous.'

Most of those, mind you, belonged to the supporting cast—as did the 18-year-old Evonne Goolagong, who played the first match of her life on the centre court. She was beaten 6–4, 6–0 by 'the impassively efficient Peaches Bartkowicz, who looks as though she has stepped from the pages of a Brontë novel'. Peaches was not all that prim. Once she was intercepted while roaming about Queen's Club in search of a reporter she wanted to thump. She was a big girl, too.

One's half-term report at that 1970 tournament contained some exciting news:

'This Wimbledon needed shaking up. It happened on Saturday, when all four men's singles and three of the eight women's singles confounded the seedings. By far the best performance was that of Roger Taylor, 28, who crushed the defending champion and firm favourite, Rod Laver, 4–6, 6–4, 6–2, 6–1 before a thrilled and thunderously delighted centre court crowd. This was the best result any British man has achieved at Wimbledon since the war and one of the most astonishing in the history of the championships.

The 31-year-old Laver was unusually sharp when Wimbledon began. Perhaps he reached his peak too soon. He was disappointed ("losing isn't my nature"). He said he was not nervous ("perhaps that was the trouble") and that he was perfectly fit. But he seemed

---

slower off the mark than usual, his touch was erratic, and Taylor's floating returns lured him into a succession of errors on low backhand volleys. A double-fault and three wayward backhand volleys helped Taylor to break service to 5–4 in the second set. He was to lose only three more games.

Taylor was agile and resourceful in attack and defence. He was firm under pressure. He read Laver's game fluently. He mixed dinks and lobs, seldom offering Laver the ball at the pace and height the Australian likes.

This was the first time Taylor had beaten Laver, who has played six Wimbledon finals and won four of them. It was the first time Laver had been beaten at five Wimbledons since he lost to Neale Fraser in the 1960 final. Fraser, Taylor, and two more of Laver's bogies, Tony Roche and Ismael el Shafei, are all left-handers. It was the first time Laver had been beaten in a major championship since he lost to Cliff Drysdale in the 1968 United States open championship. Then, as on Saturday, Laver's service was not what we expect of the world's finest player.'

And so on. But the reverberations of Taylor's triumph were not entirely welcome on court two, where another British player was defying the seedings. Winnie Shaw beat Kerry Melville 6–2, 6–4:

'Taylor has never played better. Nor has the 23-year-old Miss Shaw, who simultaneously was beating the fourth seed, Miss Melville. Miss Shaw has had difficult draws at Wimbledon and has never before been past the third round. On Saturday, from the knock-up onwards there was distracting noise from the centre court and from the thousands, on the promenade and around her own court, who were watching Taylor's progress on the flickering electric scoreboard.

"It was a bit off-putting," said Miss Shaw. "Everybody kept cheering and cheering, and it obviously wasn't for us." When Taylor won, there was an explosive din, someone threw a coat in the air, and Miss Shaw double-faulted.'

Let us extract a segment from my report of a match that induced Ken Rosewall to say: 'That's as good as I can play':

'Rosewall gave Tony Roche 10 years and beat him 10–8, 6–1, 4–6, 6–2. The 47-minute first set was the finest of the championships. Rosewall's performance overall marked him as part magician, part ordinary mortal, and all tennis player.

The first set had a gorgeous, thrilling beauty. These are players with touch and flair, quick wits and imagination. They spread richly coloured, flowing patterns across the length and width of the court. They played cat and mouse. If they had as much fun as the rest of us, they had the time of their lives.'

John Newcombe—a smart match-player whose forehand volley and second service inspired a respect that amounted to awe—beat Rosewall in the first five-set final since Ted Schroeder beat Jaroslav Drobny in 1949. The women's final was difficult to assess because one could only speculate about the effects of Mrs Court's damaged left ankle (it was strapped up, and she had been given pain-killing injections) and Mrs King's troublesome right knee. But these two extracts are adequate reminders that it was quite a match:

'Margaret Court, 27, became Wimbledon champion for the third time by beating Billie Jean King 14–12, 11–9 in two hours and 27 minutes in a final that will be remembered as one of the greatest women's matches played anywhere.

It had a thrilling beauty that chilled the blood and, in retrospect, still chills the blood. It was the longest women's singles final in the history of the championships: and the first set was the longest played by either sex in a Wimbledon singles final.'

And later:

'There is a temptation to look for a flaw in the texture of all great deeds—sporting, literary, artistic, or what you will. To succumb to that temptation for a moment, the only thing this match lacked was a sharp contrast in style and character. It had everything else in abundance. It was so good that it challenged belief. It still does.

Here were two gloriously gifted players at their best, or so close to it that the margin was irrelevant. They gave us a marvellous blend of athleticism and skill, courage and concentration, experience and wit. They moved each other about with remorseless haste. They hit a flashing stream of lovely shots. The match was punctuated throughout by rallies of wondrously varied patterns.

But the bright colours of the day were never meretricious. Every stroke, every tactical shift, was neatly tailored to the need of the moment. This was thoroughly professional tennis, the best the women's game could hope to produce.'

The introduction of the tie-break had little effect on the 1971 championships. Mrs Court was beaten in the first all-Australian women's singles final but had some excuse because it transpired that she was pregnant at the time. The tournament as a whole inspired me to explore the garden of prose with even more enthusiasm than usual. Maybe that was the year I switched from beer to wine. With apologies for another reference to 'thrilling' beauty' (haste often breeds clichés) here are a few extracted chunks:

On Rod Laver beating Tom Okker:

'Laver's efficiency level looked about 80 per cent: and he gave the impression that he knows where to find the other 20 per cent when he needs it. We noticed anew the lazily self-conscious walk, the blurred lightning of reflexes, footwork, and control of the racket head. We noticed the playful good humour, the hair tossing amid the swirling breezes of the centre court. We noticed the running forehands clouted from under the noses of spectators in the front row, the startling whip of that top-spin backhand, the capacity to hit gloriously aggressive shots when logic suggested defensive thinking.

With Okker an admirable foil, here was a fine match between two whippy, swift and restlessly adventurous welterweights. Their tennis was all timing, touch, and improvisation. Their shots continually stepped with dainty tread on the frontier between the brave and the reckless. Okker, waiting to receive service, pawed the ground like some colt eager for a gallop. Adversity eventually lent wings to his assurance. But when it mattered most he was a man trying to snatch sunbeams out of the air.'

On Billie Jean King beating Christine Janes (neé Truman):

'Christine Janes, defeated on the centre court, was a housewife and mother revisiting the playground of her youth for some healthy exercise with an old but younger rival. The friends of the 60s were still around her; still strong in their affections, but no longer expecting too much from a woman who seems at last to have discarded the label of the eternal schoolgirl. They were applauding a memory rather than nourishing a hope.

Mrs King is still at her peak, whereas Mrs Janes has descended to the relaxing warmth of the valleys, where she can smell the urban flowers and look back on high endeavour without regret for the challenge that was yesterday.

... For a while the crowd dreamed and roared. That was all: but it was enough. An old friend had sung us a few lines from a well remembered song.'

On Ken Rosewall beating Cliff Richey:

'Had this match been written as fiction, we would not have believed it. It began at 3.30. After 94 minutes Rosewall was two sets down and looked sad and worn and tired—not in his limbs, but in his mind. At 7.15 he had the first of five match points. At 7.28 he won: with a backhand down the line played so calmly that this might have been some practice match.

Richey climbed slowly and painfully over the net to shake Rosewall's hand. Two huge crowds roared ovations—the crowd inside and the crowd watching the flickering digits of the electric scoreboard on the promenade. Those ovations rang and rang through the twilight of Wimbledon.

... Here were the boxer and the fighter, the artist and the craftsman, the old matador and the young bull. The one was hotly combative, the other coolly surgical. Yet in the sharpness of contrast they were as one: quick little men with good ground strokes, a taste for lobs, and an unyielding competitive spirit.

The patterns they weaved covered the length and breadth of the court. They hit drives like bullets and lobs that had a precise and delicate beauty. They explored the angles with a subtle delight in the game's aesthetic possibilities. They used bluff and double-bluff. At times each drew the other to and fro like a puppet.

... All the time, you felt the match was trembling in the balance. Rosewall, desperately, was trying to fit together the wayward pieces of his game. Could he do it in time? We know the answer now. But at the time all was glorious uncertainty as one thrilling rally succeeded another. Richey reminded us that he will work until he drops—and then get up and work some more. But gradually, marvellously, we saw magic settle on Rosewall.'

On John Newcombe beating Colin Dibley:

'Newcombe has such supreme confidence in his strength, sense and skill that any opponent must begin to doubt himself. Newcombe's is the kind of face that emerges victoriously through smoke and dust and a sudden flutter of flags at the end of those battle films. He kept baring his teeth, puffing out his chest, and looking fierce. To pass the time between Dibley's double-faults, Newcombe mopped his brow and rearranged his muscles.

It was all too much for Dibley. In his first full season on the circuit, here he was playing the Wimbledon champion on the centre court. He had the slightly bemused air of some part-time footballer who suddenly finds himself marking George Best at Wembley, and cannot understand how it happened.'

On Margaret Court beating Judy Dalton:

'Mrs Court and Mrs Dalton, both big and robust, forthright and aggressive, played a match that was all Australian steaks and sunshine. They clouted their services and drives to the lines. They did not so much hit their volleys as inter them. This was no match for softies. Mrs Dalton beat Mrs Court at Wimbledon in 1968. It was nice to see her back on the centre court with the old engaging swagger and a new red ribbon.'

On the men's semi-finals:

'The Goliaths stood no nonsense from the Davids at Wimbledon yesterday. John Newcombe and Stan Smith, two big and brawny men whose moustaches seem utterly irrelevant as a proof of virility, qualified in straight sets for the men's singles final. Whatever happens, it will happen fast. But for the intervening obstacles, the services projected by Newcombe and Smith would endanger Channel shipping and the wildlife of Norfolk.

... Smith is 6 ft 4 in tall. He is a Private, first class, on leave from the United States Army. But with his height, erect bearing, and military-type moustache, there can have been few soldiers who looked less like Privates. He holds his racket as if it were a toothpick. He appears to hit his service from just in front of the roof of the stand. When he leaps for a lob, it is like watching some pallid monster rising from the deep.

... Newcombe, whose drooping moustache suggests that he has been to places most of us would rather avoid, played tennis of a thrilling beauty. It was as if the champion's whole life had been dedicated to the single aim of winning this particular match as fast as possible. Here was strength with finesse, power with a polish—you could see the sense shining through.'

Smith's punchbag was Tom Gorman. Newcombe's was Ken Rosewall. Newcombe then beat Smith in a five-set final. The new women's champion was Evonne Goolagong, then 19, who beat both Billie Jean King and Mrs Court in straight sets.

Mrs Court was probably the first player to visit us at home. She and Barry made a long trip to a nondescript village near High Wycombe where we had a nondescript little house. Something went disastrously wrong with the timings and dining arrangements and it has to be confessed that, as social occasions go, this one was a non-event. It was succeeded by a series of larger, better organized gatherings when we moved to a more roomy, slightly eccentric old house near Beaconsfield (all our houses seem to be 'near' somewhere). Alison and Mark Cox had to find their way to Knotty Green. So did Winnie—the former Miss Shaw—and Keith Wooldridge. But during Wimbledon my wife and I concentrated on overseas players, journalists, and officials. These naturally included some of the young ladies who made my labours on the circuit so much fun: Helen Gourlay ('Nature designed her for wine and candlelight and romantic music', as I wrote when she reached the French final); South Africa's 1972 Federation Cup heroines, Pat Pretorius, née Walkden, who developed an idiosyncratic line in banter that became tennis jargon, and the blonde and boisterous Brenda Kirk; and that rare combination of brains, brawn, and beauty, Katja Ebbinghaus, the star of an all-German guest list. All this is merely to explain that on a personal level the best feature of Wimbledon is the chance to meet so many cherished old chums—and the worst feature is that it is so difficult to find time to relax together. Eventually we dropped the dinner parties because transport arrangement became too complicated. Wherever we live is a long way from anywhere.

A bunch of special people briefly achieved prominence, in

victory or defeat, during the 1972 Wimbledon. One was Kerry Melville ('Miss Melville has lovely eyes and a heart tuned to laughter'). Another was Mary Ann Eisel, who came to Wimbledon from St Louis, where most of the leading men were competing in a World Championship Tennis tournament. Players who recognized the authority of the WCT organization, rather than that of the International Lawn Tennis Federation, were barred from Wimbledon that year. The political nonsense gouged the heart out of the men's draw. But there was an interesting and impressive newcomer called Jimmy Connors ('a square-shouldered chap with a neat fringe, a rolling gait, and a two-fisted backhand') and a joyous match between two popular men:

'The most dazzling and delightful match of the first five days was contested by two unseeded players. Jaime Fillol, who was serving for a 4–1 lead in the fifth set and had a match point at 6–5, was beaten 6–4, 7–5, 2–6, 4–6, 8–6 by Tom Gorman, the man who beat Rod Laver to reach the last four a year ago.

Fillol and Gorman have much in common. Both were born in 1946. Both graduated at university before playing tennis full-time. Both are handsome, gentle and charming men. Of either, it could reasonably be said that you could not wish to beat a nicer fellow. Both are D'Artagnans of the court: clean-limbed, athletic, fast on their feet, and playing tennis that is all flashing steel.

They seemed inspired by the setting, the sunshine, and the pleasure taken from each other's company and skill. All was fire and restlessly eager mobility. They created some lovely tennis, lacking only a sharp spice of contrasted styles. The only pity was that one of them had to lose.'

Jaime and his wife Mindy live in Santiago and collect children and dogs. They think big. At some American tournament Jaime sought my advice about buying and importing a specimen of a famous old breed. He insisted on handing over enough dollars to cover his subscription to the appropriate club. Thus it was that a Chilean tennis professional became a member of the Pyrenean Mountain Dog Club of Great Britain. Tom Gorman once told me that he had three ambitions: to go to a domestic airport and buy a ticket for the next flight (anywhere); to do the same at an international airport; and to walk into a locker room, pick up the first racket he saw, and play with it. He achieved the first ambition and landed in New Orleans. When last we met, the second ambition was still pending and so was the third, because he was then under contract to use a particular make of racket. But Tom is that sort of man. He invents his own new horizons.

The women's singles produced a match that was a feast for public and Press:

'Jack Jones sings ballads that say it all. What a lovely dream it was. If a picture paints a thousand words, then how can I paint you? If such romantic songs were written about tennis matches, they would be written about the youth and freshness and beauty of such a match as we saw on the centre court at Wimbledon yesterday. But all the records will tell us is that Evonne Goolagong beat Christine Evert 4–6, 6–3, 6–4 in 93 minutes.

To clothe those stark statistics with a few explanatory trimmings, Miss Goolagong was a set and 0–3 down but then won seven successive games at a cost of only 10 points. In the third set Miss Evert was twice a break up, but won only one of the last four games. Miss Goolagong scored the last nine points: one of them for Miss Evert with a forehand into the net. But to assess the match solely in those terms would be to assess Michelangelo's worth by the number of hours he spent painting the Sistine Chapel.

We expected this to be one of the most absorbing matches of our time. It was. For much of its course it was also one of the most accomplished, delightful and dramatic. The only virtue it lacked was that of consistently high quality. Until the second set and the match were beginning to slip away from her, Miss Goolagong was embarrassingly erratic with her forehand drives and volleys.

For the rest, the match had everything. Here were two smart and charming young women: the one, Miss Goolagong, almost 21 years old, who became champion last year at her second attempt; the other, Miss Evert, more than three years younger. At Wimbledon, as in the United States championships last September, the young lady who would rather be famous for being a girl than for being a tennis player reached the last four at her first attempt. They had not played each other before. The waiting was worth while.

That was the youth and freshness and uncertainty of the match. The beauty lay in the sharp contrast of style and character and the rich tapestry of strokes and tactics laid before us at the heart of the struggle. On the one side was the apparently casual artistry of the champion, with her capacity for treading the peaks and valleys in turn, and her greater ability to vary the pattern and pace of the rallies. On the other was the slim, trim and poker-faced Miss Evert. Her iron will insisted that everything should be in its proper place. Her chin, held high, suggested an arrogance entirely foreign to her nature.

It is often said that the best professionals are those who most consistently combine length and pace. That is the way Miss Evert played. Once she had settled into her rhythm, she gave hardly anything away. Her tight-lipped concentration and anticipation parried many of Miss Goolagong's sharpest thrusts. She was ruthless with anything loose in midcourt. She was hungry for every point. For a while her hunger was too easily satisfied.

The strategic pattern was swiftly established, with Miss Goolagong playing to the backhand and Miss Evert to the forehand: so that at times it seemed half the court was utterly irrelevant to their endeavours. Miss Evert was the first to prosper from this tactical exercise. For a long time any shot to Miss Goolagong's wayward forehand was a sound investment.

For her part Miss Goolagong showed the expected ability to draw Miss Evert to the forecourt: but was too untidy to profit from it. The shot we expected to be the most decisive of the match was Miss Goolagong's sliced cross-court backhand, exploiting the short angle and enforcing a rising return (if any) from Miss Evert's two-fisted backhand. It peeped occasionally through the clouds. But for the most part Miss Goolagong was in the shadows.

The crowd were sympathetic because they had taken Miss Goolagong to their hearts in the two previous years. The fact that she was losing mattered less than the fact that she was playing badly. How long must her and their frustrations endure? We had seen her get in and out of trouble so often that James Bond led a sheltered life by comparison. But could she do it again?

She could. Her first glorious response to adversity came when she was 2–5 and love–30 down in the first set. She won nine successive points. She lost the set anyway. But the glowing embers of her talent seemed to have been roused into flame at last. The flame died as swiftly as it had flickered: she went 0–3 down in the second set. Miss Evert was gaining assurance and gradually increasing the pressure.

That was when the floodgates opened and a foaming tide of dazzling tennis flooded upon us. That was when Miss Goolagong lost only 10 points in seven games. Suddenly, her forehand was sweetly in tune, her brain was at its sharpest, and she was leaning gracefully into her shots and taking the ball early to hustle Miss Evert out of her stride.

Trailing clouds of glory behind her, Miss Goolagong went to 1–0 in the third set. Then for a time it seemed that the match had ceased to stimulate her. But from 2–3 down the purple of majesty settled upon her again. She was always finding some inventive and daring means of ending the rallies. Those dipping, cross-court backhands were finding their mark: and the young American oak bent before the young Australian willow.

To the last, the brave and resolute Miss Evert kept pounding away. At 3–4 down she saved a break point with a raking backhand and hit two more winners to save the game. But the only other point to come her way was a gift from Miss Goolagong. In the last game Miss Goolagong hit an astonishing forehand cross-court dink when she was under such pressure that she was almost falling backwards. The last point said much for both players. Miss Evert hit a blazing cross-court backhand, but Miss Goolagong's backhand stop volley converted it into a winner.'

Meantime Rosemary Casals was 'travelling down a well-trodden road to the land of the lost' because she was playing Billie Jean King. That year, Virginia Wade was the only player to take more than six games from Mrs King. The men's singles, of course, was unusually short of class because the World Championship Tennis celebrities were not competing. But there could be no cavilling about the quality of the final. Two chunks of my report will suffice:

'We shall not forget the first time we watched a Wimbledon final on a Sunday afternoon. It was an occasion that so delighted, thrilled and bludgeoned the senses that by the end of it the nerves of players and spectators alike must have been numb. What happened, in plain terms, is that Stan Smith beat Ilie Nastase 4–6, 6–3, 6–3, 4–6, 7–5 in two hours and 41 minutes. In the skill and virtuosity of its content, the shifting patterns of its dramatic crises, the continuous sharp contrast of style and personality, it was one of the great matches of Wimbledon history.

On the one hand was Smith, 6 ft 4 in tall and sometimes known as "The Blond Bomber". On the other was a superb athlete and a gloriously resourceful stroke-player, the lank-haired Nastase, the first Rumanian to reach the final. Here were a craftsman and an artist. Here was a tingling clash of power and finesse. Here was calculated discipline opposed to whiplash flair. Yet at times each borrowed the other's virtues, so that we were often startled by Smith's subtlety or by Nastase's strength as the richly embroidered texture of the match was spread before us.

At the climax each seemed inspired by the heights to which their splendid endeavours had raised them. If they had any nerves left, those nerves were firm. If they had any doubts, those doubts were suppressed. They plundered their reduced resources for a last, desperate exchange of flashing strokes, as if aware that fortune could only favour the brave.'

Let us skip the intervening paragraphs and pick up the story at two sets all:

'The last act of the drama was upon us. For a time it seemed that cracks were appearing in Smith's heavily fortified blend of courage and will. In the fourth game he threw away an easy point with the whole wide court open to him. In the next, probably the crux of the match, 20 points sparkled this way and that—including seven game points to Smith and three break points to Nastase. Yet when every nerve end within him must have been twanging with apprehension, Smith remained cool enough to win that game with a gentle backhand drop shot.

But he was not done with adversity yet. At 4–4 he was love–30 down, at which point he hit a winning stop volley off the wood. That piece of luck must have encouraged the massive American. In the next game he had two match points but could not win them. At 5–6 down Nastase roared away to a 40–love lead, but was then afflicted by some scorching service returns and a double-fault. Smith had two more match points: and finished the job with a lob that unexpectedly induced Nastase to cut a backhand overhead into the net.

Smith flung his racket high and leapt the net. He beamed, stretched his arms to the skies, and blew a kiss to the rapturous crowd, who knew that this Sunday afternoon at Wimbledon would stay green in the memory. With one mighty hand, he held aloft the burnished trophy that is the most coveted in tennis.'

The 1972 ban on World Championship Tennis was succeeded in 1973 by the famous boycott. This time the conflict was between the Association of Tennis Professionals and the International Lawn Tennis Federation, the collective voice of the national associations. But the root causes were the same: the new breed of full-time professionals were fed up with being pushed around like pawns in a political chess game. Extracts from pieces written on three consecutive days will suffice to identify cause and effect. First:

'The basic issue is a determined and concerted effort by the ATP to establish the freedom of professional tennis players to pursue their living as and when they wish, as long as they honour their commitments (a hotly debated reservation in the Pilic case).

... The ILTF committee of management could not begin to challenge the ATP board's collective knowledge of the modern professional game. This does not mean that the ATP should govern tennis. It does mean that within their own sphere they command more respect than the ILTF and should have a bigger say in the conduct of their own affairs.'

Second day:

'Showing a formidably solid front, the Association of Tennis Professionals have collected the signatures of 71 men, including at least 12 of the 16 singles seeds, who will not play at Wimbledon unless Nikola Pilic is allowed to do so. Pilic refused to play for Yugoslavia in the Davis Cup and was suspended by his national federation. This suspension was confirmed by the International Federation, after Pilic had appealed, and his entry for Wimbledon was therefore rejected. Pilic applied to the High Court for an injunction, but this was refused after a three-day hearing.'

Third day:

'The crisis is over. The battle to make the 1973 Wimbledon championships a connoisseur's delight, as well as a sporting and social festival, has been lost. The Association of Tennis Professionals, together with their sympathizers, yesterday ripped an appalling 79-man wound in the championships.'

The reporter's task in such circumstances is to study the facts and principles involved, present a dispassionately lucid case for both sides, and then give his conclusions. I had fought many a battle, verbally and in print, on behalf of WCT, who laid the foundations for men's professional tennis as we know it today. I now did the same for the ATP, who were trying to build on those foundations. This sympathy for the ATP cause—as outlined in the first of the preceding extracts—left me pretty isolated among those writing for Britain's national dailies. It was some comfort that prominent overseas writers thought the way I did. Domestically, though, I had to take a lot of flak and was repeatedly urged (not by *The Times*) to adopt an anti-ATP stance. The boycott's effect on Wimbledon was, of course, an emotional issue in Britain. One must remember, too, that there is a great deal of 'committee reporting', a tendency for a group of writers to take a common approach to the day's news. That is the safe way, especially for newcomers to the trade. But the outstanding writers have always been those with the confidence to take an independent line which may or may not coincide with 'committee' thinking. The reporter who has to be one of the crowd can never be anything else.

My first-day report began thus:

'Ernest Ewert beat Konstantin Pugaev at Wimbledon yesterday. Things like that were happening all the time. There was a splendid sadness about this opening day. The splendour lay on the occasion: in the green beauty of the place, in the unobtrusive slickness of the organization, and in the business-as-usual crowds attracted by sunshine, social pleasures, and an affectionate eagerness to support a great sporting festival that so many had deserted. Never mind the quality, feel the width: here was the opportunity for a day out in a good cause.

The sadness lay at the heart of it all: in the anonymous mediocrity that put much of the tennis beyond the scope of serious critical appraisal. Even the spectators packed around the main courts were often respectfully yet sympathetically silent, as if visiting the sick. We shared the joy of many young men for whom playing at Wimbledon was a dream come true. But Wimbledon deserved something better.

Around the outside courts the public looked blank and vaguely puzzled, as if they had turned up at the wrong party. Strangers in white were hitting tennis balls. Had Oscar Wilde been there he would doubtless have observed that, although he could not remember the names, the manners were familiar. "What's happening?" I asked a friend.

"This could be game, set and match to what's-his-name".'

That reference to Wilde is a reminder of how helpful the dead can be in keeping one's prose alive. A hazard confronting those who write fast about the same subject almost every day is that the vocabulary tends to contract. We wear the same literary clothes too often, forgetting those at the back of the wardrobe or the bottom of a drawer. Moreover, an excess of writing can be jading. I have found three remedies. One is to leave the typewriter alone for a day or two, especially during the week before a major championship. Another is to carry around a dictionary new enough to be a guide to fashionable usage. Assuming there is time, I can check a definition and decide whether a word does the job I want it to do. The third remedy is to travel in the company of someone who can recapture for us the sparkling joys of our language—Oscar Wilde, Jane Austen, or C. E. Montague.

In 1974, Ken Rosewall kindled the fires again (his and ours). For example, Rosewall beating Roscoe Tanner:

'They talk of putting people in refrigerated boxes and preserving them for posterity. Rosewall, aged 39, has a better way. The lined face lies. His reflexes, footwork and stamina show little sign of decay. His tennis has the unfading charm of Mozart or Rembrandt or a sunset in the hills. The incredible little chap has obviously found the secret of eternal youth ... It was appropriate that Rosewall should win with a stroke that, time and again, had cut shafts of brilliance through the beginnings of twilight: a backhand volley that skimmed from the turf with an instantly dismissive authority.'

Or Rosewall beating John Newcombe:

'It was as if all Newcombe's creditors had called on him at once. To change the image, he was like a heavyweight boxer waiting patiently for an opening while some waspish welterweight peppered him with punches.

Except for the second set, that opening never appeared. In the third Newcombe scored only 12 points. Once he flung down his racket with an indignation that was understandable. He seemed to be playing half a dozen Rosewalls. All were playing well; and wherever Newcombe put the ball, one of them was bound to turn up. At times the man's statuesque helplessness was pitiful. He looked the way Samson must have felt after that famous haircut.

Rosewall seemed to regard Newcombe's fearsome service as an invitation to a party. The little man seldom looked happy on court, because he is a perfectionist beset by reminders that perfection is out of reach—in his case, only just.'

Or Rosewall winning 6–8, 4–6, 9–8, 6–1, 6–3 against Stan Smith, who had a match point in the tie-break:

'The transformation was astonishing. Having scraped through the first set, in which each had two break points, Smith visibly grew in confidence as he won the second and went to 5–3 in the third ... He looked awfully big ... He has no more muscles than anyone else. But they cover larger areas. When he extends his limbs to the limit in order to serve, it seems that yards and yards are unfolding.

... Rosewall kept looking sadly at the ground, like a man who has been presented with a dud cheque after waiting 22 years for a golden handshake ... He kept serving double-faults, too. With his service, this was like the driver of a hearse getting fined for speeding.

... A backhand volley took Rosewall to 5–all: and there was a tumultuous roar from the huge assembly as the seeming corpse, ripe for interment, sat up, blinked, and looked around him.'

And so on. That marvellous recovery made Rosewall the oldest finalist since 1912 and the only man to play in finals 20 years apart. But he lasted only 93 minutes against Jimmy Connors, the youngest men's champion since Lew Hoad beat Rosewall in 1956. In those days Philip Howard, now literary editor at *The Times*, occasionally graced our Wimbledon page with one of his delightful essays. He described Connors as 'a windmill in a hurricane'. Nice one, Philip.

In 1975 Billie Jean King won her last Wimbledon singles final by beating Evonne Cawley (née Goolagong) 6–0, 6–1 in 38 minutes, losing only 24 points. It was the most one-sided final for 24 years. After the men's quarters I made the point that Roscoe Tanner and Guillermo Vilas were not the most graceful of stylists: 'They are the kind who chop wood rather than carve it ... Vilas is a poet built like a wrestler. He uses so much top-spin that his racket seems to surround the ball rather than hit it.' Connors lambasted Tanner in a semi-final:

'Tanner began to look slightly glassy-eyed. Nobody was supposed to play tennis the way Connors was playing it. He was tearing up the textbooks and writing his own.'

Connors was playing ridiculously well. I suggested that in the final Arthur Ashe would have 'about as much cause for confidence as the Light Brigade charging the guns'. That was the common view. How wrong we were. Two extracts tell the story:

'On Saturday it seemed doubtful whether Ashe would even take a set from Connors. We suspected Connors was no longer playing matches—merely giving exhibitions. But Ashe won 6–1, 6–1, 5–7, 6–4 in two hours and five minutes. This was one of the most startling successes in the history of the championships. It was startling not because of any clear disparity in their ability but because Connors had beaten Ashe in their three previous matches and, during Wimbledon, had not lost a set, playing so well that it seemed a form of mental cruelty to send anyone out to play him.

The climax produced the most piquant surprise of the tournament, and one of the most interesting men's finals for years. Tactically, the match was fascinating. Its pattern was amazing for three-qurters of an hour, dramatic for the rest. Its outcome was uncertain to the last. But the champion was beaten. The underdog triumphed. It was a final straight out of schoolboy fiction. The bookmakers had no cause to regret their introduction to Wimbledon.

... The president of the Association of Tennis Professionals beat the game's best known "non-joiner" because his strategy was shrewdly conceived and soundly executed. It may not be an exaggeration to suggest that Ashe won the game's most famous tournament, a grass-court event, by playing the best "clay-court" tennis of his career.

Ashe gave Connors speed of shot only when the need for variety—or the chance of an outright winner—insisted on it. Even his service was usually hit at three-quarter pace, in the interests of precision. His percentage of first services was high. Many were effectively aimed at the sidelines. He teased Connors with chips and lobs. He gave him a lot of "junk" balls, as they call them. His length was superb. All was measured, calculated, unhurried. During the changeovers Ashe relaxed utterly; so still that he might have been in a trance. His self-discipline was total.

Ashe's only concession to the surface and to his natural game was his eagerness to threaten Connors from the net at every opportunity. Ashe's forehand volley, often vulnerable, was almost flawless.'

Doubles tend to be better entertainment than singles but have a raw deal in terms of prize money and publicity. Usually they are played late in the day, when clock-watching reporters are pounding away at typewriters. But on the second day of the 1976 championships I simply had to take a little time off from the Press room to watch four men who excelled at both forms of the game:

'A funny thing happened on the way to Wimbledon. They forgot to give a doubles seeding to John Newcombe and Tony Roche, five times champions and, in a sense, defending champions (they won the title the last time they played together). Thus was the tournament deprived of its logical final—those great Australians against the most consistently successful partnership in the modern game, Brian Gottfried and Raul Ramirez, the top seeds.

Never mind. The match happened anyway, glowing like a flower in the vegetable patch of the first round. Gottfried and Ramirez won it 7–9, 8–9, 9–7, 6–3, 6–4. But Newcombe and Roche proved their point, too. For almost three sets they were like hardened regular soldiers—up to all the dodges, tactical and psychological—outsmarting the most talented recruits from a new draft.

Then, just in time, the resilient younger men managed to ask a little too much of the aging legs at the other end of the court. Newcombe and Roche played the better doubles. But they could not do so for quite long enough. A deft, dazzling, spectacular match ended with a 65-second standing ovation. Whatever happens in the final it will be no better than this.'

For the second day running Adriano Panatta was on court six entertaining his compatriots and a host of adoring teenage girls:

'His foil this time was Dale Collings, aged 20, a qualifier from Queensland, who has reduced his weight to 15 st 7 lb but remains a massively flabby figure—struggling, it seems, to burst through the constraints of shirt and shorts. There is also a moustache, a lot of long hair, and a peaked cap. Collings is an extraordinary figure. They call him "The Animal" or "Big Red". Panatta beat him in five sets. But Collings served for the match at 5–4 in the fourth set.

Panatta had not crossed his path before and was doubtless over-confident, expecting some sort of rest day. Then Collings started exploding services across the net, including 26 aces and 21 double-faults. Divots came up. Panatta, the champion of Italy and France, pawed at them thoughtfully, as if hoping he might find clay underneath. He stood back. Collings aced him. He approached the service line. "Big Red" aced him again. Panatta, his face a mask, looked across the net with eyes that saw but did not believe.

A watching Australian observed that playing Collings must be like playing a whale. He looks the kind of man who keeps getting cross with James Bond ... The crisis came with that 5–4 game. The tiring Collings knew he had to win it. But his service let him down when he most needed it. Panatta hit two good returns. The Australian's chance had come and gone. Panatta took the set on a contested line decision. The players made rude gestures at each other.

But that brief show of acrimony was swiftly dispelled at the beginning of the fifth set. Collings, waiting to receive service, suddenly started waggling his hips. Can you imagine a king-sized jelly caught in a gale? If not, you cannot imagine the spectacle presented to Panatta. He shook with laughter, Collings joined in the fun and the spirit of the occasion was restored. Then the fifth seed smoothly advanced to the third round.'

Panatta had a match point against Charlie Pasarell but was beaten in five sets. Here are brief pen portraits of a man and a fifth-set incident:

'Pasarell moves so slowly between points that at times he seems to be flirting with reverse gear. He has fast eyes and hands, but is otherwise designed exclusively for leisure. His shots are like the lashes of a whip, or sudden flashes of lightning across a muggy, drowsy landscape ...

When Panatta was serving at 3–all and 30–love, there was an incident that told us much about the Italian's concern for the little things that make life so much worth the living.

A sparrow, perhaps suffering from the heat, was wandering about behind him, twittering away as sparrows do. Panatta could not concentrate. He gently rolled a ball towards the sparrow. No reaction, other than a fresh outburst of cheeping. So Panatta strolled across and picked up the sparrow in a strong yet tender hand. Panatta has a way with birds, but what to do with this one? He considered the umpire, then changed his mind and handed his fluffy bird to a spectator.'

That was the day Jimmy Connors and Ilie Nastase had a doubles to play and went on court in rugby shirts and bowler hats (removed, of course, for the match itself). When Connors was beaten by Roscoe Tanner in a straight-sets singles, it was back to nature study:

'Tanner is the kind of man who keeps ringing the bell on fairground strength machines. He served 19 aces, an average of more than one a game ... Connors must have felt like a batsman facing a succession of Lillees and Thomsons on a fast wicket. There was many a snick that would have carried to slip or gully. We looked for scorch marks across what was left of the centre court grass. Underground, worms and other subterranean livestock doubtless called hurried emergency meetings.'

That may have been the year when I was made aware that such whimsical asides were causing chuckles over the cornflakes at Royal breakfast tables. One afternoon I was sitting at the typewriter sorting out random thoughts when David Mills, then secretary to the All England Club, strolled into the Press room and said Princess Alexandra would like to meet me.

'Now?'

'Well, yes. Are you busy?'

'No. But it would hardly be respectful to turn up in a bright green beach shirt.'

David saw the point. Had I a jacket and tie with me?

'No. Tricky. You could tell her I'm in labour, pushing a deadline. Or you could tell her the truth. Play it any way you like. Perhaps, if she's still interested, we could do it tomorrow—and I'll bring a tie.'

She was and I did. Princess Alexandra's smile was slightly impish, her ice-breaking comment perfect:

'I wouldn't have minded the beach shirt.'

The Princess was fun (and dishy, too). Later I gathered that, if bored by the tennis, she sometimes spread seeds of panic among the security staff by wandering off in uncharted directions and

chatting to anybody who happened to be obscuring the wallpaper.

The 1976 championships were in their 10th day before the spirit
of enchantment settled on a centre court singles. The players
concerned were Ilie Nastase and Raul Ramirez, two clay-court
experts:

'The joy of these two lay in their assured delicacy of touch, in
their gift for bluff and cunning improvization, in their command
of spin, in the quickness of their wits and footwork. The semi-
final round is a serious occasion. Yet Nastase and Ramirez imbued
it with laughter; not by playing the fool, but by a mutual indulgence in the teasing, tantalising physical chess more commonly
associated with Roland Garros and the Foro Italico ... The taste
of vin blanc cassis and Frascati was briefly revived on the palate
of the mind.'

When Bjorn Borg beat Guillermo Vilas I wrote that Borg 'ran
like a deer, leapt about as if on springs, and served and smashed
like a low-flying bomber'. Borg became the first Swede to win the
title and the first man since Chuck McKinley, in 1963, to become
champion without losing a set. He had an ailing stomach muscle,
took cortisone injections, and sprayed his stomach with a cooling
aerosol at every changeover. Yet his speed was astonishing. In the
final Nastase 'was mostly inhibited, cautious and, often, negative.'
That match probably marked the end of Nastase as a serious
contender for major championships. The competitive confidence
had drained out of him.

There was a teasing, swirling wind on the day of the women's
semi-finals. Chris Evert took three sets and 85 minutes to beat
Martina Navratilova:

'Miss Navratilova is more demonstrative, less predictable.
Groundless though the fear might be, one would never be 100 per
cent certain that, if the waiter spilt the soup, she would not sock

him with the spoon. Yet here she was, having luckily survived intimidating crises against Françoise Durr and Susan Barker, convincing us that within a year or two she could be mature enough to win Wimbledon.

. . . She charges the net like a ship under full sail with a following gale. Her smashes and volleys are the kind that punctuate a rally with a full stop rather than a comma (assuming she remembers, on a windy day, that the ball may try to sneak off in another direction before she can biff it).'

Virginia Wade could make nothing of Evonne Cawley and the wind:

'The Australian was so light on her feet that she reminded us of those television commercials in which some glamorous model in a nightie flits along a twilit shore without making visible contact with the beach. She arrived at the net as if by magic, rather than by leg-work.'

In a two-hour final Miss Evert beat Mrs Cawley, who had won all four of their previous matches on grass. In the course of a 1,600-word assault on the typewriter I suggested:

'Miss Evert popped into the tennis circuit like an off-the-peg dress that fitted perfectly. True, the dress had a label on it: "Heavy duty material unsuitable for fast courts." But yesterday Miss Evert ripped off the label and emerged, indisputably, as a player who can beat anybody on anything.'

Miss Wade's turn came in 1977: at the 16th attempt, when she was nine days short of her 32nd birthday. She beat Betty Stove in the first over-30s final since 1913. Miss Wade is intensely patriotic and has a strong sense of history, so it was appropriate that she should become champion in Wimbledon's centenary year in the presence of the Queen—who was celebrating the 25th anniversary of her accession and had not been to Wimbledon since 1962, when Miss Wade first competed. This was all so neatly coincidental that it might have been scripted. The final, in fact, was more predictable than the semi-final in which Miss Wade played inspired tennis to beat Miss Evert. The public could hardly believe what they were seeing:

'The crowd were strangely subdued. They had come to Wimbledon, most of them, expecting a snack—and found themselves sitting down to a patriotic feast. There were murmurs of pleasurable surprise. They were happy but dared not make it too obvious, in case the gods who had spread the treat before them should suddenly take it away.'

And at the end of the final:

'What a roar there was, what a raging sea of hands. A minute passed before the umpire, dutifully observing the last rites, could announce the score. Then the Queen came on court—the monarch of a realm greeting the monarch of a sport ... Flags waved everywhere ... Hurrahs rang round the centre court.'

John McEnroe made his Wimbledon debut and became the first qualifier and the youngest player to reach the last four. He was beaten by Jimmy Connors, who then took Bjorn Borg to five sets in a final that, eventually, was marvellously exciting. Borg said he had never been so tired on a tennis court. No wonder. Connors would not have been prescribed as a rest cure after a semi-final described in *The Times* under the headline 'Three hours of summer lightning'. That analogy appeared in my story. But reporters do not write headlines. That has to be done in the office. After a page has been planned (designed) the sub-editor handling each story must devise a headline to fit a set length. The 'letter count' is also conditioned by the kind and size of type that best accords with the overall page plan. In this case the headline was in perfect harmony with the nature of the report, most of which is given here:

'Borg's 6–4, 3–6, 6–3, 3–6, 8–6 win over Vitas Gerulaitis in three hours and four minutes was a Wimbledon classic—challenging the glittering memory of Stan Smith's win over Ilie Nastase in the 1972 final ...

A year ago Gerulaitis beat Arthur Ashe, who was then the reigning champion. Yesterday he almost did the same again. In the fifth set he had a point for a 4–2 lead but stayed back on his service and, when he eventually charged to the net, was off the mark with a forehand volley. Both men later agreed that this point was critical. Borg broke back for 3–all instead of going 2–4 down.

In the 11th game Borg, serving, three times heard the umpire call "deuce". Again the champion was teetering on the brink of a plunge to oblivion. But three games later, somehow mustering his drained resources for a huge effort, he set about Gerulaitis's service and broke through for the match. A lob, cruel in its perfection, reduced Gerulaitis to 15–40 down. On the next point he attacked— which is in his nature in any situation and was essential now— but again misdirected a forehand volley. Different versions of the same shot, the forehand volley, thus let Gerulaitis down.

In the way of statistics, those will suffice. Beauty should be enjoyed, not measured. But how to describe this sample, save in terms of three dazzling hours of summer lightning? On the whole, grass-court tennis is not the best. But during matches such as this (if only they happened more often) it achieves a splendour that cannot be surpassed ...

A reasonable man would not think it possible for two tennis players to maintain such precision at such high speed under such pressure over such a long period. The sustained quickness of footwork, reactions, and racket control was astonishing. It mat-tered not that—save for Borg's rocking walk, his headband, and his two-fisted backhand—he and Gerulaitis might have been bro-thers. They gave us plenty of variety: drops and lobs, sudden changes of pace and angle, to punctuate all the whirling, pounding agility and aggression. At times the geometry they created almost happened too fast to be properly savoured. Yet the entire match was dominated by earned points: in a context that insisted there must be a host of hasty errors.

These two know each other well. They are friends and practise together. Their personalities are complementary—Borg the intro-vert, Gerulaitis the extrovert. Gerulaitis, at 22 a year the senior, was born in Brooklyn of Lithuanian stock and popped over to Europe earlier this year to win the Italian championship on clay. He is wealthy enough to indulge a taste for fast, expensive cars. He owns two Rolls-Royces, a Mercedes and a Porsche. But car or no car, the man has powers of acceleration no other tennis player exceeds.

Gerulaitis put the accelerator flat down at 4.55 and kept it there until 7.59. He kept dashing to the net and relying on his quick reactions to deal with anything Borg threw his way. Gerulaitis was gambler and acrobat in one. When he opened up the court and put away a winner, he often held the pose for a moment—grinning, relishing the joy of a moment in time. When serving, he made none of the fashionable fuss. He just looked at Borg: then aimed and fired.

Borg was younger, but looked older. They say he has ice in his veins. He certainly needed something like it yesterday. The storm Gerulaitis blew up was intimidating. Often Borg was on the baseline, quietly preparing a stroke when there was no warning of danger: and suddenly there came into his peripheral vision the figure of Gerulaitis, bounding eagerly to the net with his blond hair flowing.

But Borg never flinched, never showed the slightest sign that his nerve was weakening. He said later that he was so anxious to reach the final that he was a little nervous, a little inhibited about hitting hard. But he always had more soundness and versatility in his ground strokes and, eventually, the composure to recoil from adversity to triumph ...

Except for the fact that neither man served exceptionally well, this was a perfect example of grass-court tennis at its best. We shall never know how Borg and Gerulaitis kept it up. But we were grateful that they did: and we shall remember them. The final can be no better.'

Frank Rostron, who preceded Ian Barnes as *Daily Express* tennis correspondent, often said that he was paid to write about tennis—not to watch it. There is truth in that. The Borg–Gerulaitis match, for example, overlapped most of our deadlines. I doubt if I saw more than half of it, because I was too busy at the typewriter. Deadlines or no deadlines, it is impossible to see everything. Whereas football and rugby reporters watch one match and must make the most of it, tennis reporters often spend nine or 10 hours a day gathering information on a sequence of matches played on a dozen or more courts. That is a stimulating, sometimes nerve-racking challenge. The Press help one another by exchanging information. Other sources include players, friends, court officials, and scoresheets. But basically there is no substitute for a hell of a lot of leg-work. Somebody once asked me to identify the prime requisites of a good reporter on such tough assignments as the Olympics and Wimbledon. Off the cuff, I went for fitness, enthusiasm, and a reliable wristwatch.

In 1978 Tom Okker beat Ilie Nastase in a charming quarter-final that inspired a few fancy phrases about 'The Flying Dutchman':

'Okker tends to get bored when swapping shots with violent heavyweights who ruin the texture of tennis by finishing rallies—one way or another—before they have a chance to get interesting ... Throughout a match, he maintains tactile communion with the strings of his racket, an indispensable ally. He plucks away at it like a gardener caressing plants and cajoling them to splendour ... He indulges his impatience by taking the ball early, using the half-volley from preference rather than necessity. His top-spun forehand is like a signature. Yesterday, his passing shots were like lashes from a whip, his volleyed drops like cursory last spadefuls of soil on the graves of points.'

Bjorn Borg again beat Jimmy Connors in the final, this time more easily. This was one of Borg's finest match-winning performances and made him the first man since Fred Perry to become Wimbledon champion for a third consecutive year. Perry went on court to congratulate him, and said later: 'Everything went Borg's way today. If he'd fallen out of a 45-storey window in a New York skyscraper, he would have gone straight up'. Martina Navratilova's first Wimbledon singles title offered a further historic parallel: another Czechoslovak refugee, Jaroslav Drobny, won Wimbledon in 1954.

For most of 1979 an industrial dispute kept *The Times* off the breakfast tables. During that awful interregnum I spent a lot of time with a rucksack on my back, tramping the hills and dales. Few such books have been more thoroughly researched than *The Peak District Companion*. More pertinently, I reported the major championships for a variety of weekly or monthly publications, mostly American. But the excitement of writing against the clock to meet daily deadlines was missing—and I missed it badly. That year's Wimbledon had some unusual features, summarized in these extracts from a guest editorial for *Inside Women's Tennis*:

'There was Billie Jean King raising her tally of Wimbledon championships to the record total of 20—only 24 hours after the death of Elizabeth Ryan, who had shared the record on 19 and died with that distinction intact, after spending the last day of her life at Wimbledon. There was Martina Navratilova, retaining her title after being reunited with her mother for the first time in almost four years. At a more trivial level there was a startling spectacle many would wish to erase from the memory, pretending it never happened—Linda Siegel's low-cut dress briefly failing in its policy of containment.

... Bjorn Borg became the first player since Rod Laver to win the men's singles title four times and the first since Tony Wilding of New Zealand (1910–13) to win it four times in a row. For the first time since 1921 (when Suzanne Lenglen and Bill Tilden did not have to "play through" because the challenge round was still in force) both singles champions retained their titles.

... There were six sets of brothers in the doubles, three husband and wife teams (and a brother and sister) in the mixed, and 11 of the 16 men's singles seeds failed to benefit from their protected places.'

An experiment with electronic line monitors was an interesting feature of the 1980 championships. Ultimately, though, more exciting landmarks demanded notice:

'The Wimbledon championships, deranged and bedraggled by persistent rain, could hardly have finished in greater splendour. The men's singles final was a marvellous match: one of the most exciting there has ever been and, for most of its three hours and 53 minutes, astonishing in its sustained quality. An hour and 17 minutes after having reached the first of his eight match points, Bjorn Borg beat John McEnroe 1–6, 7–5, 6–3, 6–7, 8–6. It was Borg's longest and most arduous final.

This was Borg's 35th consecutive singles win at Wimbledon (a record) and earned him his fifth consecutive championship—a feat surpassed only by William Renshaw almost 100 years ago when tennis was an amateur game still in its cradle. That is a measure of Borg's overwhelming stature: and a measure, too, of McEnroe, at 21 almost three years his junior, who was confronting the inimitable challenge of a Wimbledon singles final for the first time.

We shall remember the brilliant treasures these two shared with us. We shall remember, too, the triumph of Evonne Cawley—the first mother to win the title for 66 years, the only player except Bill Tilden to regain a Wimbledon singles championship after an interval of nine years, and the first player to win a Wimbledon singles title in a tie-break game.'

The tie-break embedded in the memory, though, was that which ended the fourth set of the men's final. It consisted of 34 desperately exciting points, a sequence in which Borg had five match points and McEnroe seven set points:

'The players' ground strokes were so fierce that, as each in turn flung himself in vain at passing shots, Borg tumbled head over heels and, two points later, McEnroe went flat on his face. This was violently exciting tennis in which each man made terrible demands on heart and muscles and sinews. The speed of shots and reactions, and the racket-handling and timing, were breathtaking. McEnroe had been booed onto the court. At the end he was given an echoing ovation—because he had played like a man and behaved like a man. He had lost a tennis match, but in terms of public acclaim he had won Wimbledon.'

In 1981 McEnroe won the title but loused up the public relations job, both on and off court. In reaching the final, Borg came back from two sets down:

'Bjorn Borg, champion for five consecutive years, beat Jimmy Connors 0–6, 4–6, 6–3, 6–0, 6–4 in three hours and 18 minutes at Wimbledon yesterday evening. The fact that this put Borg in the final seemed irrelevant by comparison with the blazing beauty Borg and Connors cast upon the centre court. This was one of the greatest singles matches played at Wimbledon.

It was not so much the swing of the score, this way and that.

It was not so much the clash of wills—the bleak looks that indicated both apprehension and a willingness to make a straight choice between a VC or a blanket. What ennobled the match was the quality of the tennis and the skill and spirit that provoked it.

... In the first set Borg scored only 13 points. Connors, "Jimmy the Grunt", is still the most exciting player in the game ... It did not seem possible that one man could have so much energy and spend it so freely. There seemed to be a swarm of Connors on court—all of them racing about like lunatics and belting the daylights out of Borg.

... But one of the secrets of the genuine champions, in any sport, is that they can soak up punishment and bounce back to their best form. Borg did this ... From Connors's point of view the trouble with Borg was that he kept serving aces. Altogether Borg served 16. Serving aces is not the most obvious feature of Borg's game. Nor are his stop volleys—but it was one such that finally won him this tremulously exciting match.'

Borg's awesome dominance of Wimbledon—five consecutive championships and 41 consecutive singles wins—was brought to an end when McEnroe beat him 4–6, 7–6, 7–6, 6–4 in three hours and 22 minutes. But McEnroe's status as champion (and, consequently, as a model for the young) could not be unreservedly welcomed. In addition to his on-court outbursts, he caused embarrassment by missing the formal 'champions' dinner and also allowed himself to be baited into hot-tempered indiscretions at a Press conference. Chaos ensued. A British journalist punched an American and at one time nine journalists were milling about, some of them on the floor. I'm usually too busy, watching tennis or writing about it, to attend such conferences. I missed this fracas—and was startled by the readiness with which a few relatives and friends assumed I had started it. On such occasions one is granted the wish expressed by Robert Burns: 'O wad some Pow'r the giftie gie us, To see oursels as others see us!'

Sunday play, tolerated as an expedient in 1972 and 1973, was scheduled for the first time in 1982. Borg did not play. He had refused to accept a grand prix rule that compromised the principle behind the 1973 boycott: the principle that players should be free to play when and where they wished. Wimbledon was also wretchedly wet. One memorable feature was that Billie Jean King, aged 38, became the oldest player for 62 years to contest a women's singles semi-final. She kept Chris Lloyd (née Evert) on court for more than two hours:

'Mrs King liberally poured into those two hours everything she had learned and everything she had to give. As if she suspected that this might be her last big party, she rummaged through the cupboards of memory for all the best china and silverware. Here was all the natural wit, all the acquired tactical wisdom, all the competitive steel, and all the versatile skills she could command— notably some of the finest volleying ever to grace women's tennis.'

Another superb volleyer, Johan Kriek, played McEnroe that day:

'There is less than 5 ft 8 in of Kriek but most of it seems to consist of muscles and springs. In short, he bounces and bulges … His mind impulsively leads him down some strange by-ways. He fell twice; once flat on his face, when he suddenly began to go through swimming motions—the crawl. The second time he decided to vent his frustrations by doing a handstand. Kriek kept talking to himself and, when receiving service, spun his racket as if using a manual foodmixer.'

Connors, champion eight years earlier, regained the title by beating McEnroe in a final that lasted four hours and a quarter. The winner's performance was marvellous but the match was not:

'McEnroe was more than six years the younger man. But he could not serve well enough to subdue a lion-hearted opponent whose physical and mental stamina lasted far longer than logic suggested was reasonable ... Everybody loves a fighter. Connors is a popular champion because he gives 100 per cent and threatens to break himself into pieces in the effort to give more.'

The 1983 championships basked in sunshine and produced some delightful tennis. Much of it was played in a spirit reminiscent of the days when—as Mark Cox once put it to me—people went on the circuit because they wanted to play tennis, whereas many of today's breed go on the circuit to make money. Trey Waltke exemplified the mood of nostalgia by playing in cricket flannels. At 18 Andrea Jaeger became the youngest competitor since Maureen Connolly to reach the women's singles final. At 39 Mrs King again advanced to the last four—and also contested the most attractive final of the tournament. That wrapped up the mixed event, in which John Lloyd became the first Englishman since 1936 to grab a piece of a Wimbledon championship. The other piece went to that nimble, jolly Australian, Wendy Turnbull. There were many sparkling matches, among them Kevin Curren v Tim Mayotte, Curren v Chris Lewis, Vitas Gerulaitis v Ramesh Krishnan, Mrs King v Beth Herr, and Carling Bassett v Andrea Temesvari. Curren, remember, served 33 aces in disposing of Connors. Then he played Mayotte:

'Kevin Curren, who is such a serene character that his coach affectionately calls him "Unconscious", beat Tim Mayotte 4–6, 7–6, 6–2, 7–6 in two hours and 55 minutes at Wimbledon yesterday in one of those matches that will be remembered as much for the players as the play. The match was contested in the best spirit and after a finish highly charged with excitement Mayotte clapped the winner as they approached the net for the handshake. Then Curren put his arm round the loser.

Here were two mutually appreciative sportsmen who had enjoyed a good scrap and were left in no doubt—the crowd stood to give them a long ovation—that in taking pleasure from the game and each other's company they had also given pleasure to thousands of others. They reminded us, too, of what should be a truism: playing a game for a living is no cause for getting cross ...'

In the last few games an aura of greatness settled upon this exemplary demonstration of grass-court tennis:

'Earlier, each man had relaxed for a moment or two, between points, to savour the humour of the luck that swung this way and that. But nobody was relaxing now. Even the sun came out, enhancing the heat of the battle on the centre court.

In the tie-break Curren led by six points to three: three match points. Mayotte saved them all—one with the help of the net cord. Then Curren finished him, reaching match point again with a forehand service return that challenged belief and, finally, serving a winner to the backhand. The entertainment was over; but two handsome young men had played marvellous tennis and, in the process, had restored our faith in all that is best in professional tennis.'

After that, it said much for Curren's next match that I thought it 'the most exhilarating of the championships'. Here is the introduction, plus two extracts:

'Chris Lewis beat Kevin Curren 6–7, 6–4, 7–6, 6–7, 8–6 in three hours and three-quarters at Wimbledon last evening to become the first New Zealander to reach the men's singles final since 1914 (Anthony Wilding) and the first unseeded player to do so since 1967 (Wilhelm Bungert).

... Curren, jaded by a heavy programme of singles and doubles, somehow found reserves of strength and energy to lead 3–0 in the fifth set. Lewis drew level. Each in turn flung himself headlong in the course of astonishingly acrobatic rallies. Curren even played a shot on his knees.

. . . What a pity it was that either had to lose. But Curren has the game to reach the final some other day, whereas Lewis, one suspects, may never have a chance like this again. It remains to be seen how much fire will still be burning within him when he goes on court with McEnroe.'

That line of thinking turned out to be sound. Curren was to reach the final in 1985. Lewis was a second round loser in 1984 and 1985. And in that 1983 final he could do nothing about McEnroe. There had been no more one-sided final since John Newcombe beat Bungert in 1967. And Martina Navratilova beat Miss Jaeger in the most one-sided women's final since 1975. Miss Navratilova can sometimes be edgy but on this occasion 'her skirt came unwrapped in the first game and the shared laughter instantly settled her nerves'. Which leads me to another embarrassing moment . . .

The Duchess of Gloucester is quite a tennis fan, and pretty with it. We first met during a Wightman Cup match at the Albert Hall. After that 1983 Wimbledon my wife and I were invited to Kensington Palace for drinks and canapés. The long drive was awfully hot. I walked and watered the dogs and we left them in the paddock under the shade of a tree. While my wife smartened up in the ducal bathroom, an affable chap in shirt sleeves made me welcome in the garden. We chatted about this and that, mostly gardens, until an influx of guests evidently demanded his attention. As he turned away I said:

'I'm sorry. We weren't introduced. I didn't catch your name'.

'The Duke of Gloucester'.

'Oh. Would you like me to go outside and start again?'

He neatly let me off the hook by suggesting, modestly, that there was no reason why his wife's guests should recognize him, or vice versa. But at the end of the soirée, when we said our thank-yous, there was a twinkle of mischief in the Duke's eyes as he smiled and said:

'I hope you came across one or two familiar faces.'

Game, set and match to the Duke of Gloucester.

Dukes in shirt sleeves can be disorienting. On a particularly hot afternoon during the 1984 championships the Duke of Kent stood up and doffed his jacket—whereupon there was a roar of incredulous laughter from the adjacent Press and public as half the men in the Royal Box instantly followed suit. Pavlov's theory of the conditioned reflex was still making sense. Those championships presented an interesting professional challenge. *The Times* was wrestling with new technology and earlier deadlines. I could not be sure that matches would finish in time for the first edition. By way of insurance, it seemed a good idea to concentrate on the players as people, on impressions rather than match-analysis. But the first day was no problem:

'Ivan Lendl, who is seeded to play John McEnroe in the final, had a usefully prolonged but worrying match in the first round at Wimbledon yesterday. He took two hours and 17 minutes to beat Dick Stockton 4–6, 6–0, 6–3, 5–7, 6–4 in the breezy depths of court one.

This was the same Stockton who beat Ilie Nastase and Alex Metreveli to advance unseeded to the semi-finals 10 years ago. The same Stockton who reached the French semi-finals in 1978. The same Stockton who had so much bother with his back that it was no surprise when he withdrew from serious competition in singles. This was only his third singles match since August.

In the recent French championships Lendl won the singles and Stockton fell off some shelf in the memory to share the mixed doubles title with Anne Smith. When the Wimbledon draw was made, it was suggested here that, even with 33 birthdays behind him, Stockton "may have one good match left in him". He had indeed.

Stockton comes from Dallas. He is a big, quiet man who walks carefully and watchfully, with a slight loose-armed stoop as if expecting a challenge to a fast draw. The curvature of his legs suggests that they have spent long hours wrapped around a horse. There is an air of calculated violence about him, even between rallies.

Stockton hits hard, volleys the ball as if intent on burying it, and exploits the short angles like a doubles expert—which he is. He uses his wealth of experience to create gaps on the other side of the net and hide those on his own side.

During the first set, especially, Stockton gave Lendl something of a lesson in the craft of grass-court tennis in general and volleying in particular. When a backhand down the line gave Stockton a break to 3–2, a cloud passed over Lendl's face. Those deeply set eyes seemed to recede even further. Lendl looked rather unusual, anyway—has that once-dark hair been given a mild dose of henna?

Stockton held his service for 4–2 and in the process chased a lob, turned on it, and passed Lendl with a cross-court backhand that clipped the net cord. Lendl sank to his knees as if punched on the button. In that set Stockton demonstrated that he was once—and for a while, still could be—a better grass-court player than Lendl.

Then Lendl overpowered him for two sets before Stockton, now playing from memory, bounced off the ropes at a time when he should have been asking no more from life than a shower and a rest. Even in the fifth set, when the spring had gone from his legs, Stockton still raised doubts about the outcome. This was a good match for both men: Lendl because of what he learned and Stockton because of what he remembered.'

What a comfort it was to have a match like that as a first day 'lead'. Later in the same report I tried to capture fleeting images of scattered matches:

'On court 17 Rodney Harmon, a tall man whose permanently questioning look suggests that he expects nothing but the unexpected, took five sets to beat a bouncy little Spaniard, Emilio Sanchez.

... Lloyd beat Andreas Maurer over five sets, but Dowdeswell lost to Ben Testerman in three. The latter match seemed to have a hair-raising effect on the young lady operating the scoreboard. Or was it just one of those "punk" coiffures?'

Wimbledon was rich in character that year—ideal for a reporter with a bent for impressionism. Take Sherwood Stewart, for example:

'Stewart is a large man with receding hairline and a light beard, which means that his contemplative mien is totally framed in an oval of hair.'

Or another first-round loser:

'... that quivering bundle of energy called Raffaella Reggi, who plays as if plugged into the electricity system. When "Raffi" goes out of a tournament, it is as if someone had switched out the lights on a Christmas tree.'

Or a more general theme:

'There was a good deal of grass-crushing pounding from big men with big feet. The alarm bells were doubtless ringing in that unseen underworld populated by creatures that burrow and crawl in the daily chore of survival. Upstairs, as it were, the sun was shining, seeded players were in action on 11 of the 18 courts, and there was still room enough to wander about in a world of legwork and handshakes and scattered dramas.

Tim Mayotte raised an interesting point during one of those

---

press conferences at which players bare their souls—and sometimes their teeth, too. The courts were drier than usual, he said, and could soon "tear up".

Let the ground staff worry about that. The rest of us know very well that England is a dry country at present. The potatoes are not coming along all that well, are they? But as far as Wimbledon is concerned the ground-stroke specialists should have more of a chance than usual. That means better tennis. To hell with the potatoes.'

Paul Annacone beat Mark Dickson:

'Dickson is a quiet, genial man, but takes so long about the business of serving (does he think the permitted 30 seconds interval is an obligation that has to be met in full?) that his departure from a tournament does no harm to its entertainment value.

Yesterday Dickson wore the familiar yellow and white baseball cap that gives him something to fiddle with during the long, ritualistic pauses that precede scattered outbursts of violence. These were rather too scattered to do him much good against Annacone, who achieved similar effects with less fuss and more accuracy.'

At the opposite end of the premises (you have no idea how we reporters scurry about!) a more interesting match was in progress:

'Mark Kratzmann, aged 18, a left-handed country boy from Australia, took the 13th seed, Tomas Smid, to five sets in three hours and 11 minutes—and came within two points of winning. Left-handed country boys from Australia are not to be taken lightly and the fair-haired Kratzmann has much in common with another of the breed, Rod Laver ... The match contained a moment of startling comedy when Smid snicked a Kratzmann service to leg slip. The ball went first bounce through the open doorway of the first aid room. Shock treatment for the ailing.'

Lendl had an easy win over Derek Tarr but was briefly held up when some birds had a domestic squabble in the forecourt:

'Lendl flourished his racket at them, then reached into his pocket and tossed the intruders some sawdust. Affronted by this dietary insult, they left—and Lendl waved them goodbye. A colleague who should be ashamed of himself suggested that never before had Lendl been Tarred and feathered in the course of one match.

Lendl later expressed mock resentment at the fact that his photograph on page three of *The Sun* had not been given the prominence usually accorded to photographs on that page. Straight-faced, he said he would take some injections and come back next year.'

But that first week was not all comedy:

'McEnroe? He won. But he carried on his trivial private war with courtside microphones on the ground that bad language would be no problem if such microphones were banished. Has it occurred to him that the microphones would not matter if he cleaned up his act?'

A note on birds:

'Like an eagle swooping on its prey, Miss Mandlikova was all swift, predatory elegance. She moved well, timed her shots perfectly, and played with such graceful facility that her tennis achieved a dazzling, almost frightening beauty.'

Carina Karlsson, even more bird-like than Hana Mandlikova, was one of two fledgling professionals to take wing:

'The dreams were fun while they lasted and will linger in the memory. Moreover, a sunny afternoon on the centre court at Wimbledon was no bad time to wake up. It happened yesterday to Carina Karlsson and Paul Annacone, who were newcomers to the championships, had to qualify, but advanced to the quarter-finals. Then Miss Karlsson had to share a court with Chris Lloyd and, later, Annacone took on Jimmy Connors.

... Miss Karlsson, the first qualifier to progress to the last eight of the women's singles, and Annacone, the first to reach the men's quarter-finals since John McEnroe in 1977, have impressed us not merely with their tennis but also with their engaging personalities. They would be pleasant company around the house, though Annacone might fall asleep and Miss Karlsson looks capable of knocking over any obtrusive item of furniture.

... Mrs Lloyd had the air of a dishy but rather severe governess. Miss Karlsson was like a boisterous, fun-loving child who could not believe that life was being so good to her.'

Mrs Lloyd's tennis was 'an object lesson in how to hurt people without touching them'; and Annacone's 'wealth of inexperience was evident':

'Connors and the grass made everything happen too fast for Annacone—a big, handsome man who exudes virility but was delightfully casual in his approach to the violent business of grass-court tennis. When Americans invented the description "laid back" they invented it for people like the quiet, contemplative Annacone.

Annacone's response to the speed of Connors' returns, plus the speed of grass, was often a sudden stiffening of posture, with his head jerking backwards. Imagine a Minor Counties batsman promoted to deal with West Indian bouncers, and you have the picture. When volleying, there was a strange, instant stillness about Annacone—the man and the racket—as if he had been arrested in time.'

That was a day rich in character—or a day, maybe, when I was particularly sensitive to it:

'John McEnroe, who beat John Sadri 6–3, 6–3, 6–1, did not play tennis. He composed it. He turned prose into poetry. But McEnroe's marvellous gift for dextrous improvization was hardly necessary. Everyone has difficulty reading McEnroe's game and Sadri was often hopelessly at a loss in trying to.

Sadri looked stern and had a parade-ground bearing. He was like a marine (straight-backed, short back and sides) on a mission he did not expect to survive. His tennis was soldierly, too: insistent on discipline and planning. But McEnroe does not play tennis that way. McEnroe makes his own music. Sadri was a classical artist in the alien environment of a jazz club. Somebody had stolen the sheet music.'

Martina Navratilova's progress to her fifth singles championship was illuminated by a clash with the lean, long-limbed Kathy Jordan, a somewhat frantic competitor. Miss Jordan could never be mistaken for anybody else:

'She has a frying-pan grip, a technique that does not lean heavily on the harsh principles of orthodoxy. But the important thing is where she puts the ball, not how she does it. Her racket arm bears not only a wristlet but also an elbow bandage, which means that the arm looks rather like a lagged cold-water pipe.

... The match was punctuated by roars of applause from court one, where a doubles match was in progress. That was frustrating. Reporters tend to be locked in a private world of typewriters and telephones at a time when distant ovations tell us that something spectacular is happening in doubles. Then well-meaning friends with smiling faces pop in to tell us we have missed the best match of the day. This is an example of Sod's Law.'

A reader's letter asked me to define Sod's Law. I have two favourite definitions. First, when nothing can go wrong, something will. Second, no matter how you approach a telephone box, the door will always be on another side.

In the men's semi-finals McEnroe beat Pat Cash and Connors beat Ivan Lendl. 'McEnroe,' I wrote, 'had the air of a master bored by mastery.' Connors had more trouble with Lendl, who was still learning his trade on grass, but learning fast:

'Connors was throwing himself all over the place, as if this was his last afternoon on earth and he wanted to live every minute of it to the full. He flung himself into the line of Lendl's services like a suicidal acrobat, yet repeatedly contrived returns that were perfectly timed. The speed of Connors' reactions, notably when returning service or when hurtling to and fro in the forecourt, was often breathtaking.

When working for openings, Connors swung the ball from corner to corner—somehow finding patches of accelerating grass on the worn surface—with drives like shafts of sunlight. Poor Lendl was pestered by a succession of yorkers—shots that threatened to rearrange the structure of his ankles and, consequently, were awfully difficult to return adequately.

While Connors was breaking service in the first game of the fourth set, they took a breather—each of them leaning on the net as if chatting over the garden wall. Well, by that time the match had become a social occasion, anyway.'

Unfortunately for Connors there was one more match to play:

'John McEnroe took only an hour and 20 minutes to crush Jimmy Connors by the embarrassing margin of 6–1, 6–1, 6–2 in

There was Billie-Jean King raising her tally of Wimbledon championships to the record total of 20 – only 24 hours after the death of Elizabeth Ryan, who had shared the record on 19 and died with that distinction intact, after spending the last day of her life at Wimbledon.

It had a thrilling beauty that chilled the blood and, in retrospect, still chills the blood ... It was so good it challenged belief. It still does ... Here were two gloriously gifted players at their best, or so close to it that the margin was irrelevant. They gave us a marvellous blend of athleticism and skill, courage and concentration, experience and wit.

Court (left) v King, 1970 Wimbledon final, 14–12, 11–9, 2 hrs 27 mins.

What a roar there was, what a raging sea of hands. A minute passed
before the umpire, dutifully observing the last rites, could announce
the score. Then the Queen came on court – the monarch of a realm
greeting the monarch of a sport ... Flags waved everywhere ...
Hurrahs rang round the centre court.

Virginia Wade on winning the ladies' singles in Wimbledon's
centenary, 1977.

Rosewall is a quick and quiet man, so cool, so calculating, that even his strides between rallies seem to be measured to an inch.

Laver (left) thus became the first player in the history of the game to win two grand slams, the first to win an open grand slam, and the first to earn $100,000 from a year's tennis.

Smith flung his racket high and leapt the net. He beamed, stretched his arms to the skies, and blew a kiss to the rapturous crowd, who knew that this Sunday afternoon at Wimbledon would stay green in the memory.

Smith v Nastase, 1972 final, 4–6, 6–3, 6–3, 4–6, 7–5.

Taylor was agile and resourceful in attack and defence. He was firm under pressure. He read Laver's game fluently. He mixed dinks and lobs, seldom offering Laver the ball at the pace and height the Australian likes.

Taylor v Laver, 1970 Wimbledon. 4–6, 6–4, 6–2, 6–1.

Among the men who climb to high places there is a saying that the mountains bring you three things – men, battle, and beauty. The men are true, the battle is the only kind worth fighting, and the beauty is life. Rosewall and Pasarell took us to the mountains yesterday – and the air was like wine.

Rosewall v Pasarell (left), 1968 Wimbledon, 7–9, 6–1, 6–8, 6–2, 6–3, 3 hrs 54 mins.

Gerulaitis put the accelerator flat down at 4.55 and kept it there until 7.59. He kept dashing to the net and relying on his quick reactions to deal with anything Borg threw his way. Gerulaitis was gambler and acrobat in one. When he opened up the court and put away a winner, he often held the pose for a moment – grinning, relishing the joy of a moment in time.

Borg v Gerulaitis, 1977 Wimbledon semi-final, 6–4, 3–6, 6–3, 3–6, 8–6, 3 hrs 4 mins.

Everyone loves a fighter. Connors is a popular champion because
he gives 100 per cent and threatens to break himself into pieces in the
effort to give more.

Connors v McEnroe, 1982 Wimbledon final, 3–6, 6–3, 6–7, 7–6, 6–4,
4 hrs 15 mins.

Mrs Lloyd took two hours and 52 minutes to beat Martina
Navratilova, 6–3, 6–7, 7–5 in what was probably the best
women's final I have seen here in 25 years. It took the mind back
to 1973, when Margaret Court beat Mrs Lloyd, then Miss Evert, by 6–
7, 7–6, 6–4. In that final too, Mrs Lloyd was playing a great athlete
with intimidating physical advantages.

Lloyd v Navratilova, Paris 1985.

As a woman and as a player she has grown up to a point at which she can look adversity in the face without flinching, without looking for excuses, without any undue erosion of self-assurance.

Mandlikova (above) v Navratilova, Final, New York, 1985. 7–6, 1–6, 7–6.

Martina Navratilova became the first player, man or woman, to achieve concurrent grand slams in singles and doubles ... She showed us a dazzling cornucopia of skills – the most beautiful demonstrations of women's tennis I have seen in 25 years on the circuit. The diversity of expertise on view was breathtaking.

Navratilova v Lloyd, Paris 1984, 6–3, 6–1.

That was the youth and freshness and uncertainty of the match. The beauty lay in the sharp contrast of style and character and the rich tapestry of strokes and tactics laid before us at the heart of the struggle.

Goolagong (left) v Evert, Wimbledon, 1972. 4–6, 6–3, 6–4.

Had there been an award for the best supporting actress that year, it would have gone to Gabriela Sabatini, aged 15, a dark-haired beauty from Buenos Aires. She was beaten 6–4, 6–1 by Mrs Lloyd in a semi-final but for 12 games looked born to play starring roles. After that she could hit and run no longer and therefore tried to shorten the rallies. She succeeded, but at her own expense.

Lloyd v Sabatini, semi-final, Paris 1985.

The Swedes are delightful: fine sportsmen who get on with the job
without fussing (except Jarryd, who often seems close to a nervous
breakdown) and talk about the game themselves with no hint of
either conceit or false modesty. The sleepiest of the lot is Nystrom,
who beat Becker, 6–3, 6–4, 4–6, 6–4 in two hours and 43 minutes
on Monday evening and thus cancelled the Becker–McEnroe clash . . .

Nystrom (above) v Becker, New York 1985.

The court became scarred and pock-marked as Wilander reminded the strong-armed German that playing shots is not the same thing as playing tennis. To put it another way, Becker played draughts while Wilander played chess – always thinking one or two moves ahead.

Wilander v Becker, Paris 1985. 6–3, 6–2, 6–1.

The fact that this put Borg in the final seemed irrelevant by comparison with the blazing beauty Borg and Connors cast upon the centre court. This was one of the greatest singles matches played at Wimbledon.

Borg v Connors, semi-final, Wimbledon, 1981, 0–6, 4–6, 6–3, 6–0, 6–4, 3 hrs 18 mins.

... Becker was flinging his racket at the ball as if he expected neither to come back. He was also doing his celebrated imitation of a man cycling down a cobbled street without a bicycle. Becker pumps himself up, as they say, and makes no secret of his intense excitement and iron will.

Becker v Curren final, Wimbledon 1985, 6–3, 6–7, 7–6, 6–4, 3 hrs 18 mins.

... This was violently exciting tennis in which each man made terrible demands on heart and muscles and sinews. The speed of shots and reactions, and the racket-handling and timing, were breathtaking.

McEnroe had been booed onto the court. At the end he was given an echoing ovation – because he had played like a man and behaved like a man. He had lost a tennis match, but in terms of public acclaim he had won Wimbledon.

Borg v McEnroe, Wimbledon, 1980, 1–6, 7–5, 6–3, 6–7, 8–6.

... On the other was a superb athlete and a gloriously resourceful stroke-player, the lank-haired Nastase, the first Romanian to reach the final. Here were a craftsman and an artist. Here was a tingling clash of power and finesse. Here was calculated discipline opposed to whiplash flair.

Smith v Nastase, final, Wimbledon 1972.

And when we think of Forest Hills, we shall select only the good books from the library of the mind – the tennis, the friends, and the bookstore and pizza parlour down the road.

(The Press Box) ... is a long way from the tennis and has a glass front that takes the full glare of the afternoon sun – less welcome to working journalists than it might be to tomato plants. I often dictate articles while lying on the floor in the shade under the desk. Yes, they made mistakes at Flushing Meadow.

the men's singles final at Wimbledon yesterday. This was the most one-sided final since 1938, when Donald Budge beat Bunny Austin 6–1, 6–0, 6–3. Coincidentally, 1938 was the last year in which an American retained the men's title at Wimbledon.'

McEnroe was on target with almost 75 per cent of his first services and in other ways, too, played one of his finest matches:

'McEnroe is deceptive, difficult to "read", because he can take the ball early or late and deftly commands a variety of spin and pace. His anticipation and reactions are so fast that he seems to make time stand still. On yesterday's evidence he is also a mind reader (the mind being Connors') and can be in two places at once.

An example of the latter quality occurred when McEnroe fell when advancing to the net. Connors carefully popped the ball into the open court. Just a formality. But McEnroe was waiting—a perfect facsimile of the McEnroe who was lying on the ground yards away—and hit a winner down the line.

The only other point to be made concerns McEnroe's uncanny rapport with the lines. His touch was so assured, his placing of the ball so precise, that at times one had the illusion that the lines were moving in order to accommodate him. Yesterday, McEnroe was an illusionist rather than a tennis player.'

Reporters sometimes confront the challenge of turning a dull but important subject into a good 'read'. In October of that year, 1984, I was driving to Wimbledon for a press conference concerning the annual financial statement. Was it possible to wrap up the basic facts in a package of banter? The following piece took the mickey out of everyone, including the writer (unless the championships are in progress, I sometimes wear a suit and tie when visiting Wimbledon):

'The Wimbledon championships produced a record surplus of

£4,252,193, an increase of 55 per cent on last year's £2,751,154. "Buzzer" Hadingham, the dapper and breezy chairman of the management committee, said yesterday: "We were pretty lucky, because we had marvellous weather and record crowds." The surplus goes to the Lawn Tennis Association for the greater good of British tennis.

Hadingham made the customary polite protest about the fact that the LTA would lose about £1,310,000 of the surplus in corporation tax. Jim Cochrane, the avuncular president of the LTA council, said much of the balance would be devoted to development and schools ("development" is a popular multi-purpose word with the LTA) and added that an expensive director of coaching would be appointed within a few weeks.

The LTA seems to appoint chiefs more readily than they recruit Indians. But they can now put more money into regional development schemes and, later, hope to add county tennis centres to the existing network of regional centres. And there will be extra funds, instantly, for loans to clubs.

As usual, this Wimbledon press conference was ritualistic and relentlessly genteel. Sunshine streamed through the windows across the inevitably green furnishings and the inevitably suited and tied assembly. All England Club ties were evident, even among the press corps. Are there drama critics, one wonders, who belong to Equity? True, a serenely Polish journalist was tieless, the BBC neckwear was hidden under a crew-neck sweater, and *The Guardian* served a double-fault with a reddish tartan shirt gashed by what looked like pendant mustard. The rest of us played the game by wearing the expected uniform—which makes everyone feel secure because conformityy of clothing encourages conformity of thinking. At Wimbledon, people who wear their independence are regarded as eccentric and potentially difficult.

The top table was embellished by cards identifying Mr Christopher Gorringe, Mr Jim Cochrane, Mr R. E. Hadingham (nobody knows what the initials represent), Mr John Curry, and

Mr Tony Hughes. The repetitive "Mr" seemed a broad hint to those of us lumbered with the chore of drawing up the Birthday Honours list.

Coffee was served to wake everyone up and, an hour later, sherry was provided as a sedative for those mentally disturbed by the mass of figures that formed the main course. The press were given copies of the accounts and an explanatory statement. The latter was read out by Gorringe, innocently implying that although he was literate, he was none too sure that the literati of Fleet Street were similarly accomplished.

We read, and heard, that the heaviest item of expenditure was the £2,071,705 devoted to improving the premises. Broadcasting and television fees made up £5,986,043 (a jump of £1,989,393) of Wimbledon's total income, £9,934,158. In the United States championships, the preferences of television bosses have a ludicrous effect on the scheduling. But Wimbledon, Hadingham insisted yesterday, will not dance to the TV tune. Presumably he hopes they will play it again anyway.

When we had been laid low by the financial report, the Wimbledon chairman tossed us provocative crumbs in response to supplementary questions. "The worst thing that could happen to tennis," he said, "would be a standardized surface throughout the world." Agreed. But you and I could reasonably debate his belief that a player who hits a lucky winner off the net cord should say "Sorry!" Does he advocate public insincerity as a sop to the unlucky?

It was a cosy and comforting occasion, for all that. Once again, Wimbledon has done us proud. Yet one's final thought for the day was a teasing paradox. Britain can obviously make money out of tennis players. If only we could make tennis players out of money.'

The 1985 championships were enlivened by a refreshing stream of little known heroes, heroines, and 'bit' players. After the fifth day, relevant comment was necessary:

'The early series of matches suggested that a generation had been wiped out. The courts were peopled by so many unfamiliar players with strange names that the programme might have been fictional. No pairing challenged belief more than that of Mustard and Flur, who played on what Americans call a "field" court. Make up your own vegetarian jokes.'

Todd Nelson demanded an introduction:

'Nelson is coffee-coloured (medium roast) and has such well developed muscles that one wonders how his skin takes the strain.'

So did Slobodan Zivojinovic, who beat Mats Wilander:

'(Zivojinovic) weighs more than 14 st and punches his weight. But he also has a delectable touch—you know how gentle giants can be—on volleyed drops ... Zivojinovic served 15 aces and 13 double-faults. Once he had warmed up, his service might reasonably have qualified under the legal definition of an offensive weapon. It says much for the resilience of modern stringing that Wilander's racket was never reduced to a frame with tattered appendages ... Zivojinovic's double-faults were so spectacular that, however they were noted on the score-sheet, they scored psychological points. Moreover, the draught may have given Wilander a stiff neck.

The penultimate point of the first set was probably unique for Wimbledon. Wilander, drawn wide, hit a scorching backhand down the line, a marvellous shot except for the fact that it flashed through a small aperture between the upper corner of the net and the net post. That is not allowed (not that any player, even Ken Rosewall, would back himself to hit such a diminutive target). Maybe Wimbledon should hunt around for wider nets.'

Next day there was another—even more obvious—departure from the norm:

'There was an extraordinary spectacle on court two when Pamela Shriver, seeded fifth, was confronted by the slender and leggy Anne White, who was clothed from neck to ankles in a white body stocking—the sort of thing speed skaters wear. One had visions of Ophelia coming up from the first dunking.'

That match was suspended overnight, resuming with Miss White conventionally clad:

'Wimbledon did not permit her to wear the same clothing yesterday. They insisted that she expose her legs, which seem to go on for ever but could not honestly be described as boring.'

Another two-day match was that in which Boris Becker beat Hank Pfister and, later, modestly told us that he was looking forward to 'not being a nobody'. He did not have long to wait ... Meantime we enjoyed the labours of others: for example, Miloslav Mecir, who was beaten by Tom Gullikson:

'Mecir can be a wizard on shale courts ... On grass, though, Mecir has no time to do his thing. He is an easy-going chap with no taste for doing anything in a hurry.

Mecir likes fishing. He is a big, lightly bearded man who always looks sleepy. His demeanour suggests that, having shaved and dressed in the morning, he probably feels that he has had as much exercise as he can take in one day. On court he sometimes serves underarm when his arm and his heart get weary.

It was fun watching this dreamy Czechoslovak—treading an alien surface and fighting many of his natural instincts—set about a man who knows what grass-court tennis is all about. Mecir certainly had a go. He threw himself this way and that. He skidded. He fell. He walked around on his knees for a while, implying that he was too tired to get up and, instead, might as well do a Toulouse-Lautrec imitation.

A charming, spectacular match had an appropriate ending, with Mecir sprawling on the ground again, looking puzzled and resigned as a desperate forehand went out of court. He may have mused that grass was not for tennis. It was simply something you sat on while fishing.'

The perfect contrast was Mike Leach, beating Wojtek Fibak on a court just in front of the food village (fish and chips £1.50):

'Leach is a left-hander with calf-length socks. He has a fierce service and, having dispatched it, changes character. When winding up, Leach looks a placid, reasonable man. But once the ball has left his racket Leach charges to the forecourt as if afflicted by a mild form of electrocution. His limbs jerk about all over the place. He seems to rush the net from several differnt directions at once, which must be very confusing for whoever happens to be standing at the other end.'

Another, better left-hander, Henri Leconte, beat Ivan Lendl:

'Lendl, in fact, was bewildered, demoralized and ultimately reduced to helpless desperation by an opponent who played like a whirlwind ... Like Laver, Leconte is quick on his feet, does wondrous things on the backhand, and has no taste for compromise. He insists on living dangerously. Tennis is not worth playing, he reckons, unless it is an adventure.

... Lendl likes an ordered, settled world of conventional patterns and rhythms. Leconte's company slams the door on all that. He jumps about like a firecracker on the hazy frontier between genius and madness. Leconte plays jazz—hot jazz. By contrast, Lendl's tennis is Wagnerian.'

One day I noted that Leconte's compatriot, Pascale Paradis, was 'just a vowel short of supreme bliss'. Another musical analogy—

this time neither jazz nor Wagner—came to mind while Barbara Potter was beating Jo Durie:

'Miss Potter is a left-hander with an enviable variety of services, all of them good. She tends to strike soldierly poses. One thinks of Miss Potter in terms of Sousa marches and of Miss Durie in terms of Vaughan Williams.'

If one's senses are all functioning, and alert to character and mood and imagery, tennis at this level is never dull. Have we not referred, in the last few minutes, to coffee, Ophelia, fishing, electrocution, music, and paradise? A naturalist chum, David Tomlinson of *Country Life*, extended the boundaries of tennis education even farther when he told me—it was the second Monday, the day Elizabeth Smylie beat Hana Mandlikova—that in addition to everything else he always enjoyed Wimbledon because of the local prevalence of the stag beetle, the biggest in Britain. What riches lie scattered around us. There is all of life in tennis, if we look closely. Only bores can be bored. Not that there was much chance of being bored once those 1985 championships had emerged from the rain:

'The violent storm that hit Wimbledon at 2 o'clock yesterday afternoon must have seemed kid's stuff to Jimmy Connors compared with what happened later. Kevin Curren served 17 aces and beat him 6–2, 6–2, 6–1 in an hour and 32 minutes. In Curren's 12 service games Connors scored only 16 points. Connors had only one break point—and Curren aced him.

The result meant that in consecutive matches Curren had beaten the past two champions, John McEnroe and Connors, at a total cost of only 13 games. Connors is no mug when it comes to returning service. But he spent much of the match throwing himself at shadows in the memory.

The remorseless bludgeoning he took from Curren's service put

Connors under so much mental stress that this was probably the reason for otherwise inexplicable errors on easy shots. You know how a batsman, having survived a torrid over from a fast bowler, often gets himself out to a relatively friendly spinner at the other end. A similar message came through with echoing clarity whenever Connors muffed a shot that, by his standards, should have been child's play.'

That was the day Becker and Anders Jarryd were rained off after they had split sets:

'Jarryd is more excitable than any of the other leading Swedes. He used to play a game called bandy and his legs have the appropriate curvature. Jarryd is addicted to news bulletins, statistics, Cling Eastwood, and pasta. He also has a girl friend who works for SAS, which sounds alarming but is, in fact, no more than the airline.

Becker, commonly known as "Boom-Boom", could loosely be described as a hit man from Heidelberg. Except for an exemplary volleying touch when exploring the short angles, he depends on power and fast reactions.'

Before that match was over Jarryd must have wondered if the other SAS, Britain's élite fighting corps, could have been rougher company than Becker. So to the climax:

'It really happened. Boris Becker, aged 17 years and seven months, became Wimbledon champion at only the second attempt when he beat Kevin Curren 6–3, 6–7, 7–6, 6–4 in three hours and 18 minutes yesterday, on one of the loveliest afternoons of what passes for an English summer. Becker is the first German, the first unseeded player, and the youngest competitor to win the men's singles championship.

With all those extraordinary facts jumping around in the mind, one vaguely wondered what excesses the authors of schoolboy fiction will be driven to in the future. Becker has changed the formula. There has been nothing like this before and even Becker cannot make it happen again. And just to think that a few years ago we were doubtful if any teenage tennis player would ever match the feats of Bjorn Borg.

... Becker was hurling himself all over the place and flinging his racket at the ball as if he expected neither to come back. He was also doing his now celebrated imitation of a man cycling down a cobbled street without a bicycle. Becker pumps himself up, as they say, and makes no secret of his intense excitement and iron will.'

Martina Navratilova became the first woman since Helen Wills Moody to become champion four years running. Kathy Jordan and Elizabeth Smylie won the women's doubles by beating Miss Navratilova and Pam Shriver, who had won 109 consecutive matches. In the men's doubles Heinz Gunthardt became the first Swiss and Balazs Taroczy the first Hungarian to win a Wimbledon title. But perhaps the most extraordinary feature of the tournament was that the men's champion was even younger than the junior champion. Thus was a fairytale completed and history made.

Call this, if you like, the German chapter—because it began with Wilhelm Bungert and ended with Boris Becker.

CHAPTER THREE

Flushing Meadow: A TV Game Show

THEY WERE playing a Wightman Cup match at Cleveland, probably in 1967, when I learned that the American language can be a communications hazard. Frank Rostron, then with the *Daily Express*, called his office one day and asked to be put through to the sports desk. The line was briefly silent during the process of connection and the American operator came back to him: 'Are you through?' Frank said he was—and she cut him off, because in the US 'through' means 'finished'.

This is no place for an Anglo-American glossary. All that needs to be said is that our 'common' language is a trap for the unwary. British newcomers often find the US unexpectedly alien, which makes it more exciting. The cultural bond is strong, but no stronger than that between the nations of western Europe, which are huddled together on the other side of the Atlantic. In the US I always feel European, rather than specifically British.

Working trips to the US have been a joyous education. As an example, I happened to be in Philadelphia in 1971 when Joe Frazier was training for one of his fights with Muhammad Ali. Frazier uttered one of those great truths that should be engraved on the hearts of all athletes in training: 'I feel like I'm in top shape. But the more shape I get in, the harder I gotta work to get in better shape.' And for down-to-earth humility amid the glamour and razzmatazz of showbusiness it was hard to beat the example of Ken Rosewall in Dallas a few months later. Rosewall and Rod Laver were to play the final of the first World Championship

Tennis showpiece tournament, a lavishly promoted event that brought professional tennis in from the cold. They were staying in a palatial hotel—the kind that books such entertainers as Jack Jones and Peggy Lee—and could have had anything they wanted 'on the house', from restaurant or room service. But one day Judith Elian of *L'Equipe* (Paris) and I were caught in the rain while shopping, sought refuge in a department store—and found 50 per cent of the biggest act in town sitting at a refreshment counter with the hoi polloi. Introducing Rosewall at a banquet, I suggested he could hit a $100 bill with his backhand though it would be out of character if he left a $100 bill lying around. I had called Kenny to clear that. But he never minded jokes about his thrifty habits ('as long as you don't come on too strong').

John Newcombe gave me problems in Dallas one year. He lost in the first round and inevitably threw a party. It was no use protesting that I had to get up early in order to work (one writes early in the US, because of the time difference). 'Newc' is big and persuasive. When we emerged, the empty beer bottles stood in line for 20 yards up the hotel corridor—both sides. That morning, it was like typing with gloves on. 'Next time you throw a party,' I told him, 'for Christ's sake reach the final first.' He did, too. That was in 1974, when Newcombe beat the 17-year-old Bjorn Borg in the final and said afterwards: 'When I call home I speak to my kids. When he calls home he speaks to his parents.' That 1974 Dallas, by the way, introduced a trend-setting electronic device to help the service-line judges. WCT did a lot of pioneering work.

A fast-talking promoter called Bill Riordan, who has a gift for trenchant wisecracks, made little Salisbury (Maryland edition) a big name in tennis. In 1972 he invited three European writers to fly down there after reporting the rival tournament run by Marilyn and Ed Fernberger in Philadelphia. 'I've been working here five years,' said the girl at the PanAm office, 'and nobody ever asked for a ticket to Salisbury. Now three of you. What the hell's

happening down there?' We had to go to Baltimore to pick up
Allegheny Commuter Flight 16, which could take 15 passengers
at a pinch. That trip over Chesapeake Bay is known as the 'white
knuckle' flight, especially on windy days. It was a windy day.
Judith Elian and Rino Tommasi, an Italian free-lance, held hands
across the aisle. We did a U-turn over some trees, landed, and
summoned a taxi.

'I think we go back by train,' said Rino, relieved to be down.

'We ain't got no trains, Bud,' said the taxi-driver. We used a
taxi three times that day. It was always the same taxi, the same
driver. Salisbury is a small town. The biggest thing that happened
there was the tennis tournament. The second biggest was a chicken
festival. We moved in just after a convention of watermelon and
sweet potato growers. In the local civic centre the tennis was
punctuated by popping noises from popcorn poppers. There was
snow and ice that week, too. Judith and I left early because we
were wary of being cut off in Salisbury. Sacrificing the excitement
of another 'white knuckle' flight in favour of a night drive over
hazardous roads, we accepted a lift from the Fernbergers and
watched the finals on television in their home near Philadelphia.
Somehow, Rino got out too. Rino is a sports writer, boxing
promoter, and statistician—and consciously charming. An American girl once told him he was not very modest. 'I look deep within
me,' said Rino, 'and see no reason to be modest.'

Salisbury also yielded another language lesson. I was leaving a
store one day when the assistant called after me: 'Come back
now!' And I did. But she was just asking me to call again some
time.

In 1974 I joined Judith, Lance Tingay (*Daily Telegraph*), and a
few more chums on an assignment in Tucson—a land of stark
mountains, desert, dust storms, saguaros, movie-makers, and Indians. Judith and I were out jogging one morning, admiring the
orange trees on a lonely road, when a grim, leather-clad Apache
turned up from nowhere. 'Morning!' I cried (being sociable, even

before breakfast). All we got in response was a rumbling, reluctant 'Ugh!' Judith enjoyed the exchange. 'My colleagues,' she said, 'will not believe this.'

Everybody I met in Tucson had been there two years. Another oddity was that a match between Cliff Drysdale and Ken Rosewall was interrupted because the light was not bad enough—the flood-lights were less effective in twilight than in darkness. Rain stopped play, too, which induced Jack Kramer (tournament chairman) to observe: 'We changed the balls and the courts to produce superb tennis. We thought we'd brought Mother Nature to her knees. Then we were double-crossed by the fastest rain in the West.' Professionally, the time difference between Arizona and London was enough to make deadlines irrelevant. Lance and I watched the evening's tennis, dined at leisure, wrote our reports, and left them with the telex operator. Too late for tomorrow's paper, we were writing for the next day's. Not exactly the fastest workers in the West.

Reg Brace (*Yorkshire Post*) was in far more of a hurry one day during the 1976 Masters tournament in Houston. He telephoned his Leeds office and got through—at least, he thought he had, because the accent on the other end of the line was familiar. Nerves on edge, blood pressure mounting, he kept bellowing 'Hello!' at some mickey-taking idiot who merely repeated the word. At least, that was how it seemed. Then the American operator came on: 'Sir, would you mind shutting up? You're talking to your own echo ...'

In 1977 a bunch of Brits invaded San Francisco for a Wightman Cup match. The place was everything it was cracked up to be. I went out to the island of Alcatraz with David Irvine (tennis correspondent of *The Guardian*). The beauty of the surrounding bay and unattainable hills must have made imprisonment all the more irksome. We learned that the confined criminals were given good food and all the tobacco they needed—because a full stomach and the sedating effect of tobacco discouraged violence. We enjoyed the fishing port, the food, the cable cars, and the jazz played by Turk Murphy and company at an establishment known as Earthquake McGoon's—where a young lady sprained an ankle while dancing. Three of us helped her back to the hotel where two of us left her serenely supine on a bed, and apologizing for being a nuisance. Next day she was limping—but smiling.

Three times in 12 months we had the luck to work at Palm Springs, which is mostly desert and mountains. Those of us with a head for it took the aerial tramway 8,500 ft up a canyon, through five life zones. During the 1978 Davis Cup final five British reporters hired a condominium and a car. The vanguard consisted of Ron Atkin (*Observer*), who looked after the breakfast fry-up; Reg Brace, who was in charge of the laundry; Nigel Clarke (*Daily Mirror*), otherwise known as 'Wheels' because he had a dodgy elbow and could manage no more than the driving; and the present writer (wake-up and breakfast coffee, plus supervision of the dishwasher). Reg and I shared a room and the first night we were woken up by a shattering crash. 'Bloody hell,' said Reg. Some transient guest had fallen through a massive glass coffee table. Next morning David Irvine arrived, jet-lagged and bleary-eyed, and was awarded the carpet-cleaning chore. David could not understand why he was instantly bundled into a car with the rest of us for a trip to the local glazier. By that time the fridge had been well stocked with wine and beer and a generous proportion was swiftly poured into David. That afternoon he was introduced to an American guest who asked if he was 'acclimated'. David swayed and blinked. Taking care with the consonants, he confessed: 'As a matter of fact I'm slightly pissed.'

David had missed the early morning scene in the garage. Reg ran into a laundry problem and appealed for help. 'Has anybody got any idea how to work a washing machine? Either it's broken or there's a button I can't find.' So we trooped into the garage, four middle-aged men in underpants, and stood thoughtfully around the recalcitrant machine. We were baffled. 'Here we are,' said Reg, 'allegedly four of the sharpest knives in journalism—and none of us knows how to make this bloody thing work.' But we gaffered it eventually. Our first day at the Davis Cup final thus began with a tricky washing machine and an urgent visit to the glazier. Did you think tennis reporting was all glamour?

It was at Palm Springs that I played doubles with, as partner, a big and boisterous black lady, a journalist from Los Angeles. She once turned to me between rallies and muttered cryptically: 'Man, it don't matter how long your pencil is—it's how well you write with it!'

Two recent recruits to the tennis writing corps—Malcolm Folley (*Daily Mail*) and my Murdoch group stablemate, Hugh Jamieson (*The Sun*)—were among the eight British scribes who played doubles for two hours in Dallas one morning in 1984. The interesting thing was that although we played on the third floor of that monstrously glassy hotel pictured on the opening shots of the 'Dallas' TV series, we played outdoors—because the courts, surrounded by a jogging lane, are on the roof of an extension to the main block. My room was on the 26th floor, reached via one of those spectacular elevators (no extra charge for the view) blistered onto an outside wall. Dallas is like that. The director of the World Championship Tennis organization, who promote the tournament, is the multi-millionaire oil tycoon, Lamar Hunt. Lamar and his wife always give a garden party on their beautiful 12 acre estate. In 1984 Bob Greene (*Associated Press*) cast appreciative eyes over the vast expanse of land and water. 'I've been to countries smaller than this,' he said. 'Norma and Lamar are the only people I know with their own zip code.'

By a roundabout route, (I just wanted to give you a broad view of tennis reporting in the US) that brings us to New York. Since 1967 my attitude to 'The Big Apple' has swung from disbelief to discovery, disenchantment, dislike and in some ways, even disgust. Can all that scurrying about at the foot of man-made canyons be good for the soul? Nature has been crushed by concrete.

The sky has almost been banished. Central Park excepted, greenery is so sparse and mostly pathetic as to seem an alien growth. Streets and sidewalks are cracked, pock-marked, and strewn with litter. Steam rises from the ventilating shafts of that subterranean hell called a subway system. The stale smell of the place often degenerates into an outright stink. There is a dreary ambience of decay and squalor. The decay is even evident in the running sores on some of the filthy down-and-outs who sleep in doorways, rummage in trash cans, and beg for dimes and quarters. The noise level is such that people become accustomed to talking loudly. If there are birds in Manhattan, one never hears them sing. People hurry by with impatient, worried faces. There are many grotesque, bulging figures—evidence of the gluttony that is the child of anxiety. On top of all that, one runs the daily risk of being mugged by men sometimes too desperate to care how much harm they do.

Mind you, I don't much like cities anyway. And even New York, a particularly hard place, provides psychological cushions to fall on. If vitality is a virtue, score one for 'The Big Apple'. Moreover, the warmth and rough friendliness of its people, their capacity for sudden kindnesses, often makes one feel guilty about detesting their city. For those who have time, there are also tempting shops and shows and museums, a wealth of memorable restaurants, and (until the last year or so) some joyously relaxing jazz spots.

Every day tends to start well, possibly after a 'wake-up' call, with breakfast in what is known as a coffee shop. Locals often order a bagel with lox (smoked salmon) and cream cheese. Eggs are served 'over easy' or 'sunny side up'. Toast comes in three varieties, whole wheat, rye, or white, and coffee in two, 'regular' (with milk) or black. These coffee shops tend to be lively and noisy: though I use one, the Electra on 2nd Avenue, that is an island of calm where one can wrestle quietly with the morning paper. Once a week, this is a particularly formidable task. On the last day of the 1985 US championships I bought the $1.25 (almost £1) Sunday issue of the *New York Times*, which had 11 sections. In order that you might be fully informed about such weighty matters, I asked a delicatessen assistant to put it on the scales. It clocked 7 lb, about the same as a heavily built Yorkshire terrier.

Later in the day a popular order among New Yorkers is pastrami (salted beef) on rye, with mustard. Before dinner you may fancy a Scotch—'on the rocks' or 'straight up'. The restaurants most familiar to the overseas tennis set are on or near 2nd Avenue or 3rd, from 50th upwards. It was in one of these, small and very French, that Katja Ebbinghaus once gave a perfect demonstration of tact. She never interrupted her escort during the sometimes challenging process of ordering—in my limited and stilted school-boy French. It was only at the end of the evening, when staff and customers were chatting together over coffee and cognac, that Katja gave rein to her fluent French.

Three Manhattan residents have been consistently kind in leading me to off-the-track dining delights. Susie Adams, who spent 10 years with that trail-blazing magazine *World Tennis*, favours a French place where a large waitress tends to burst into Piaf-like song. Stewart Brauns, a master of detail when it comes to Gilbert and Sullivan, tennis, and squash, is another chum with a taste for French cuisine. On the other hand Herbert Warren Wind of *The New Yorker* patronizes an Italian restaurant. Herbert is a gracious man with a gracious writing style—happily not restricted to his pet sport, golf. He goes in for hats known as 'coconut straws', has a knack of raising everyone's morale, and answers to 'Herb'.

In the past 19 years I have seen New York's 'trad' jazz scene flourish and wither. Gene Krupa, stuck up on a platform behind the bar, used to drum up business at the *Metropole* on Broadway. Next time I went there, Krupa had been replaced by bare-breasted dancers. For years, though, we had a lot of fun down in Greenwich Village at a place called *Your Father's Mustache* on the corner of 7th Avenue and 10th—site of that renowned jazz spot of the 1930s, *Nick's*. Most nights, *YFM* had a banjo band. Everybody sang, the beer came in pitchers, and waiters emptied ashtrays on the floor.

It could be a rough place, best regarded as group therapy with the emphasis on 'group'. I was down there with Mark Cox one evening until two girls suggested further festivities and a burly, surly chap alongside us began to look ominously hostile. We left. Evonne Goolagong and her coach, Vic Edwards, joined one of our *YFM* parties. Vic said it was the first time they had seen anything of New York except the hotel and the tennis. The big day, though, was Sunday, when the Southampton Dixie, Racing & Clambake Society Jazz Band blasted away from 5.0 to 9.0. The banjo player was a man called Connie. A later, pick-up band at the *YFM* featured Wild Bill Davison, whose restlessly watchful eyes raised images of Chicago and Prohibition. Then came the day when somebody told me it was all over and *YFM* had gone 'topless'.

During the 1960s European tennis writers—and for that matter, European players—were thin on the ground in New York. I was often out alone until the small hours but came to regard Jimmy Ryan's, on West 54th, as a home from home. The owner, Matty Walsh, became a personal friend. Between sets there was a relaxed rapport between musicians and customers. One morning, when the place closed at three o'clock, it was raining so heavily that Joe Muranyi insisted on driving the last two customers back to different hotels. Joe played clarinet on Louis Armstrong's last date and he talked to us about 'Pops'. We paused at traffic lights on Broadway, with the rain bouncing off the bonnet, the windscreen wipers thudding to and fro, and Muranyi saying quietly:'I'm not the kind who cries, but it took me weeks to get over his death. He was the original nice man.' The most evident host at Ryan's was the genial, gravel-voiced Roy Eldridge ('Little Jazz'), who looked after trumpet and vocals in much the way Armstrong used to. On drums, Eddie Locke or Freddie Moore ('Ugly Child') were always good for some fun. Some nights Max Kaminsky took over from Eldridge. A host of other fine musicians used to drift into Ryan's, just to play a set and remember their yesterdays. Conveniently, Ryan's was just behind the New York Hilton. When escorting young ladies back to some other hotel late at night, one could go into the Hilton through the back door and walk down the lobby into a taxi out front.

But Ryan's closed, too, and the joint pleasures of the expanding British press corps were diverted to *Red Blazer Too* (there was another Red Blazer) on 3rd Avenue. This was all things to all people—bar, restaurant, dance floor, and jazz band in one long room. Often we stayed late and then walked 37 blocks back to the hotel on what seemed to be rubber sidewalks. But *Red Blazer Too* closed in 1984, a year after the doors of Ryan's had been boarded up. New York was still a hard city: and in accordance with Sod's Law somebody was stealing the cushions.

My US debut, in 1967, took in Cleveland, Manchester (Massachusetts), Boston, and New York. In Boston there was a party at the home of Bud Collins, the flamboyant, wisecracking sage of American tennis writing. An excess of American-style Martinis (almost exclusively gin) eventually induced me to take out a long lease on one of the two Collins lavatories. 'We kept wondering where you were,' Bud told me next day. 'I paid periodic visits to the lavatory and you assured me, from a kneeling position, that you were all right. By that time we were all in the kitchen and Roy Emerson was playing the Italian championships—playing all the roles, male and female. He gave us Lazzarino and Pericoli and the squeals and shrieks. He even gave us the crowd. Merlo playing Tiriac was his best impression. He was bouncing off the dishwasher, getting lobs out of the sink and throwing an imaginary racket at the ice box (meanwhile he was opening the ice box from time to time to get out a Foster's lager). Roy was in a good, loose, Aussie mood.

'Reluctantly I had to leave the Italian championships every 15 minutes to see if poor Rex could join us. I was worried, because your track record wasn't as a drinker. You were having dry heaves, I guess. I said: "The guy may be dying, but you knew these British fellows—chin up, and the next thing he'll be whistling the Colonel Bogey march or something." Roy said: "Don't worry about a thing." He opened the door and there you were in what had become your customary position of obeisance to the commode. Roy just picked you up and slung you over his right shoulder like a sack of wheat and carried you away. It was a memorable evening—one of our better parties. I'm sorry you missed it ...'

'Emmo' had some gold fillings in those days and they had an odd effect on the lighting as he grinned down at the body on the floor: 'Jeese, Rex. I'd sure hate to feel the way you look.' The other good Samaritans who piled into the car with me were the Danish No. 1, Jan Leschley, the US Davis Cup captain, George MacCall, and a colleague from Fleet Street, Richard Evans, now with *Tennis Week*. A classy rescue team. As 'Emmo' laid me to rest, back in the hotel room, he said he'd got to know me better in that one night than he had done in the previous six years.

We were in Boston for the US doubles championships, which those days were played as a separate tournament. The next week, everybody moved on to Forest Hills in Queens (one of New York City's five boroughs) for the singles. The 1967 winners were the Wimbledon champions, Billie Jean King and John Newcombe, who thus completed grass-court doubles. For the second time Ann Jones of Britain was runner-up for the women's title. I was learning fast about the difficulties of reporting US tennis for a British morning paper. London was always at least five hours ahead, so one had to write a first edition story by lunch-time and a revised version by late afternoon. The better bits had to be transferred from one report to the next so that every reader had a clear overall view of what was happening. Almost 20 years on, the drill is unchanged.

In 1968 open competition happened at last. An era was ending on the *New York Times*, too. The renowned Allison Danzig, a genteel embodiment of tennis history, was moving towards retirement: and Neil Amdur, a bustling, hard-nosed news man, was ready to pick up the reins. On court, Pancho Gonzales and Torben Ulrich reminded us that, as I wrote at the time, 'the artist in a man does not die with his youth'. But both singles titles went to players under the jurisdiction of national associations as distinct from those under contract to promoters. In the women's event Virginia Wade beat Rosie Casals, Judy Tegart, Ann Jones, and Billie Jean King in straight sets, in consecutive matches, to become the first British winner since Betty Nuthall in 1930:

'At 6.20 this evening Virginia Wade, aged 23, the British Wight-man Cup player, shared a rostrum with Herman David, chairman of the All England Club, in the middle of the main stadium at Forest Hills. Miss Wade was holding a bouquet, a cup, and a silver plate. She and Mr David were both grinning broadly. It was an historic moment for tennis as a whole and for British tennis in particular.

Miss Wade had just beaten the Wimbledon champion, Billie Jean King, by 6–4, 6–2 in only 41 minutes to win the United States championship, the richest open event in this first year of open tennis. It was largely Mr David's pioneering work that trans-formed open tennis from a dream into a reality. It was certainly Britain's boldly defiant initiative of a year ago that made it possible for the professional groups to compete with everyone else in this year's major tournaments.

It was entirely appropriate that a British player and a British official should share the centre of the stage as the packed stadium rose to them on a gloriously sunny afternoon.'

And so on. The match ended at 6.12 p.m., which meant that the sports page report and a front page piece both had to be extemporized. There was no time to write. Note the use of 'Mr'. In those days *The Times* still took the view that administrators deserved a more overt show of respect than players.

The men's final also had a special importance:

'Arthur Ashe, "The Shadow", beat Tom Okker, "The Flying Dutchman", by 14–12, 5–7, 6–3, 3–6, 6–3 here this afternoon to win the first open championship of the United States. It took Ashe two hours and 36 minutes to carry his winning sequence of matches to 26 and thus write an unusual chapter in the history of the game.

The 25-year-old Ashe had never before won a major international championship. He is the first Negro to do so. He is also the first American to win a major men's singles title since Chuck McKinley won Wimbledon in 1963, and the first American to win his national championship since Tony Trabert in 1955.

... The match was decided chiefly by the fact that Ashe had the stronger service and also had no obvious weakness for Okker to attack. Otherwise there was little to choose between them and both played admirably, not least in their capacity to achieve precision at a breathtaking speed.

Yet they were at the mercy of an environment that insisted on a breakneck pace. Like so many grass-court finals this was often boring to watch—because it was played so fast that variety was restricted within strictly defined limits and subtlety was almost impossible. The game's commercial future depends largely on its power to draw more and more new customers. Such matches as this will not help.'

In 1969 the USTA imported the expertise of Mike Gibson (referee) and Owen Williams (tournament director), who had worked well together in raising the status of the South African championships. But there was nothing these two could do about the courts (the grass had only shallow roots) and the rain. Flying divots were commonplace and one day I wrote: 'The serve-and-volley route was looking more and more like a farmyard after the cows had come home on a wet day.' A hovering helicopter was used as a spin drier. On top of all that, Karen Krantzcke was stung on the lip by a bee, broke out in a rash, and had to retire. But Rod Laver's triumph in the men's singles hit all the right notes:

'Laver thus became the first player in the history of the game to win two grand slams (the singles titles of Australia, France, Wimbledon and the United States in the same year), the first to win an open grand slam, and the first to earn $100,000 from a year's tennis.'

In 1970 it was Margaret Court's turn to complete a grand slam. I missed that tournament because our golf man was already in the US and *The Times*, acutely cost-conscious in those days, decided he could report the tennis as well. That worked both ways: I twice covered major golf events in the US. In 1970 I stayed home and watched John Lloyd reach the semi-finals of Britain's junior championship. Next year, the first day at Forest Hills produced an unlikely 'intro' for our later editions:

'For the first time since seeding was introduced in 1927, the favourite has been beaten in the first round of the men's singles in the United States championships, the richest tournament in the game. Jan Kodes, the game's top man on clay because he is French champion, beat John Newcombe, Wimbledon champion and therefore top man on grass, by 2–6, 7–6, 7–6, 6–3.'

At that time a nine-point, 'sudden death' tie-break was in vogue at Forest Hills. But what a marvellous performance that was by Kodes, who despised grass courts—yet advanced to the US final and was to win Wimbledon two years later. Even Kodes, though, eventually had to take a back seat in 1971. One day I began a piece thus:

'The subway trains were packed on the way out to Forest Hills today. Everyone wanted to know if the unseeded Chris Evert of Florida, only 16 years old, could reach the women's singles final of the United States open tennis championships at her first attempt. Everyone wanted to watch her try. But she was beaten 6–3, 6–2 in an hour by Billie Jean King, three times Wimbledon champion. So the star of the show will not be on stage for the last act.

Miss Evert's run of 46 consecutive wins since February was halted in the midst of a huge crowd, estimated at 14,000, in the soaring bowl of the stadium court. The little girl from Florida had captured the imagination of the public. The emotional strain of the occasion was severe for both players. Photographers clustered around the small, introspective figure of Miss Evert every time the players changed ends. Small wonder that today she was more inhibited, made more mistakes, and was more prone to gestures of despair than she had been in her previous matches. Miss Evert had beaten Mary Ann Eisel, Françoise Durr and Lesley Hunt in turn after losing the first set to each. But now the glory had departed.

There were two disputed points in the first three games, with the crowd howling their opinions. Three of the first four games went to deuce. Mrs King was clearly apprehensive—she had been forced to retire during her only previous match with Miss Evert. But she carefully insisted on playing her usual aggressive game and towards the end she began to play it with assurance. She varied her length shrewdly, finished the rallies as quickly as discretion permitted, and denied Miss Evert the chance to maintain a rhythm.'

A bronzed Australian beauty called Kerry Melville beat Miss Evert 6–4, 6–2 in a 1972 semi-final, in which both players tastefully exploited their new freedom to wear colours other than white:

'Miss Melville is an exciting player. She hits the lines so often that we sometimes suspect she has an inbuilt reluctance to assault anything green ... Another important factor was her exemplary use of the drop shot, which either won points or created winning openings.'

One year I bumped into Kerry amid a milling throng on the main promenade at Forest Hills. We had not met for some time so I gave her a hug and murmured into an adjacent ear: 'Let's start some rumours' (an easy thing to do in the gossip shop of the tennis circuit). Kerry chuckled. She has a marvellous chuckle. During the 1972 Wimbledon I promised the two Kerrys, Melville and Harris, that I would buy them a beer—possibly one each—when we met in New York. In fact they went for soft drinks but in other respects found Jimmy Ryan's a strong brew. We were sitting a couple of yards in front of the stand when Roy Eldridge, looking them straight in the eyes, launched himself into what he called 'a novelty number'. The lyrics were hardly Gilbertian: 'Don't roll dem bloodshot eyes at me. Your eyes are like a road map. You'd better shut your peepers before they bleed to death ...' After that frontal assault from 'Little Jazz', who could be intimidated by Chris Evert?

That year Stephen Warboys, then the golden boy of British tennis, played at Forest Hills for the first time. He was stuck for a room, shared mine, and was a congenial room-mate—though I was unaccustomed to the cartoon series 'Thunderbirds' as breakfast viewing on TV. One evening Stephen called me and said a bunch of the boys were on their way to *Your Father's Mustache*. He was insistent that I join them. I checked the cast list, realized they were all out of the tournament, and changed into dripdry clothing in readiness for rowdy revelry. We put away vast quantities of beer, sang until we were hoarse, thumped one another with *YFM*'s special line in boaters, and had persistent difficulty in keeping the chairs upright. Eventually the largest waiter loomed over us: 'If you guys don't quit horsin' around I'll have to ask you to leave.' At *YFM*, such a reprimand may have been unique. Back at the hotel, I just took off my shoes and stepped under the shower to wash the beer stains out of everything else. Next morning, about 'Thunderbirds' time, I discovered an Australian Davis Cup player, Phil Dent, curled up on the floor. 'Philby' was staying out of town and the party finished so late that he hadn't been able to make it back. On the whole, 1972 was a good year.

For three years running, Australians stopped Chris Evert in the semi-finals: first Kerry Melville, then Margaret Court, then Evonne Goolagong, whose 1974 win took an awfully long time:

'Today she completed a 6–0, 6–7, 6–3 over the Wimbledon, French, Italian and South African champion, Christine Evert, who had previously won 56 consecutive singles matches. Miss Goolagong has won all their four matches on grass and was always in charge of this one. But she had to serve for the match three times and needed five match points, two of them in the second set.

Miss Goolagong led 6–0, 4–3 when an enchanting match was interrupted by rain on Friday. The players had to wait more than 45 hours before changing ends. But the match immediately regained the flowing grace and beauty, the bold expertise, and the rich tactical contrasts with which it had delighted us two days earlier.'

That extract will suffice. I have no wish to tax your patience with an excess of long reports saying the same things about the same people. But we must carve a larger slice from the last piece I wrote at Forest Hills that year:

'James Connors and Billie Jean King are the United States tennis champions. Both beat Australians in today's finals. Connors crushed Ken Rosewall by the humiliating margin of 6–1, 6–0, 6–1, in only 67 minutes. Rosewall scored only 42 points in the most one-sided final in the history of the championships. By contrast, Mrs King twice had to rebound from adversity before beating Evonne Goolagong 3–6, 6–3, 7–5. Mrs King was 0–3 down in the third set and had to serve for the match twice before winning the title for the fourth time.

Connors lost only six games to Rosewall in the Wimbledon final and today he beat him even more decisively. He is the first

American since Donald Budge in 1938, to win all three of the big grass court tournaments—the Australian, Wimbledon, and United States championships—in the same year. Another man who achieved that feat was Fred Perry, in 1934, who observed today: "A lot of people didn't believe the three sets Connors played in the final at Wimbledon. But he did it again. We are not privileged to see tennis like that too often—and we have seen it twice."

Connors served the same curried dish he cooked at Wimbledon, but this time made it even hotter ... Even when he led 5–1 in the third set he was aware, as he confessed later, that Rosewall might still beat him. So Connors kept hammering away as if his life depended on it ... He kept roaring into the attack like a highly mobile lightweight tank with no reverse gear. If he could possibly reach the ball, he did so: and having done so, he hit it as hard as he could.

Whenever possible, he took the ball early. All the time, too, he was going for the lines as if regarding them as targets rather than hazards. He fairly flung himself into his shots. Between points, he often jumped up and down on the spot, bursting with eagerness to get on with the job. He was like some boxer interrupted by the bell when thirsting for the kill. In the parlance of the ring, the fight might well have been stopped to save Rosewall from further punishment.

Rosewall went down as if from a rain of punches, hanging his head in dejection as the winners sped past him. His own best shots were often returned with interest. There was nothing he could do except reflect, perhaps, that he was nearly 40 years old and had therefore done rather well to advance to his fourth United States final in 20 years.'

Note that *The Times* of 1974 quaintly insisted on 'Christine' Evert and 'James' Connors. One has to write in accordance with current 'office style'.

In 1975 the US Lawn Tennis Association dropped the 'Lawn'

from their title and tore up many of the seemingly rootless grass courts of Forest Hills. Seven new, slate-grey shale courts were put down. These were faster than the loose-top courts of mainland Europe and seemed to me to be a sound compromise between Paris and Wimbledon. The days of easy—often lucky—points were over. Three of the last four in the men's singles were shale-court specialists and the new champions were Manuel Orantes and (it had to happen) Chris Evert. The USTA also introduced floodlights, extended play into the evenings, and discarded the unpopular 'sudden death' tie-break introduced in 1970. The star of that revolutionary 1975 show was Orantes, one of the most serene and charming chunks of humanity ever to come out of Granada:

'When we look back on this beginning of a new era at Forest Hills, the rugged, wide-smiling face of Orantes will fill the picture. At 10.40 on Saturday evening he came off court after three hours and three-quarters of thrilling combat with Vilas, who led by 6–4, 6–1, 2–6, 5–0 and had five match points. Orantes did not get to bed until three in the morning, because he could not turn off a bathroom tap and had to find a plumber. At 3.10 in the afternoon he was back on court with the defending champion, Connors, and gave him a lesson in the craft of the clay-court game.'

In 1976 Bjorn Borg had a rough time getting past Jaime Fillol, Brian Gottfried, and Orantes. And in an accomplished, memorable final—one of the most thrilling matches I have seen anywhere— Borg was not quite good enough, even on shale, to stop Jimmy Connors:

'Connors won 6–4, 3–6, 7–6, 6–4. It took him three hours and 13 minutes. But it seemed healthy, for the greater good of the game, that the bolder player, the man prepared to take chances, should emerge successfully from this mighty clash of wills.

Borg teased Connors with heavy top-spin. There were times

when Connors almost needed a step-ladder in order to reach the
high-bouncing ball and whack it back. Borg also tried a series of
small variations in length and pace and angle. He was superb at
counter-hitting, at challenging the incoming volleyer. He had
plenty of practice . . .'

The crisis came in the 69-minute third set:

'Connors had three points for a 5–2 lead. But Borg, somehow
maintaining his precision under the most ferocious barrage of
shots, took the set to a tie-break in which he had four set points.
On all those points Connors attacked successfully. Finally, on the
20th point of that tremulously exciting tie-break, Borg was off
target with a backhand down the line. That set, which gained
additional drama from a fall that left Borg with a grazed knee and
a shale-stained shirt, was neither the beginning nor the end of the
argument. But it was the crux, the nub.'

In 1977 Laurie Pignon of the *Daily Mail* rang his office one day
and, as a deadline was pressing, had more than a hint of urgency
in his voice as he asked to be put through to a copy-taker. Instead,
he got the canteen. 'I asked for a copy-taker,' he bellowed, 'not
the coffee-maker!' Laurie's reverberating and often outrageous
patter was a joyous sideshow for the Press. His telephone calls
were never private. Once he had us falling about with laughter as
he startled his distant wife with the line: 'Sorry, dear, but I haven't
been able to get you any edible knickers . . .' But Melvyn knows
how to play the Pignon game. An American operator showed
much aplomb when Laurie asked for a collect call (these must be
'person to person') to 'The Dragon' at their Sunbury-on-Thames
cottage.
Operator to Mrs Pignon: 'I have a collect call for The Dragon.'
Mrs Pignon to operator: 'Dragon Speaking.'
Laurie was a born actor and chose the role of the traditional

English eccentric. His zest for life would tax the resources of men half his age. In 1983 he retired and took up hill-walking and as I type these notes he is on his way to the highlands of north-western Scotland. With 'The Dragon', of course.

Those 1977 championships were extraordinary. They were the last played at Forest Hills and the last played on shale. They were also the first to apply the point penalty system and the first to feature Renee Richards, the transsexual. Mike Fishbach briefly rose from obscurity to the headlines with the then notorious 'spaghetti' racket. Even spectators got into the act: one sustained a mysterious gunshot wound from a stray bullet of unknown origin, another slashed his wrists while lounging by the clubhouse, and a change in the programme so angered the crowd that they tossed rubbish onto the court and refused to leave the stadium between the afternoon and evening programmes. That was the year, too, when Wendy ('Rabbit') Turnbull scuttled past Rosie Casals, Virginia Wade and Martina Navratilova into the final. In the first round Miss Wade, Wimbledon champion, had beaten Dr Richards—an astonishing coincidence because in 1960 Neale Fraser, Wimbledon champion, had beaten the same player (then Richard Raskind) in the first round of the men's singles. The Fishbach nonsense was eventually stopped by John Feaver:

'Feaver is big, muscular, highly trained, and has the stoical composure one expects of men who come from the land Thomas Hardy used to write about. Yesterday he beat Michael Fishbach of Long Island, who has leapt to prominence here by beating Billy Martin and Stan Smith and challenging everyone's credulity with a racket that has extra layers of thick stringing secured by tasselled knots. When applied to the ball his racket makes a noise like muffled footsteps in the night. The ball dips and swings all over the place. Fishbach also hits his ground strokes two-fisted on both flanks. He puzzled and beat Martin and Smith. He puzzled and almost beat Feaver.'

I wrote a farewell to Forest Hills for the next issue of the year-book *World of Tennis,* pointing out that the championships would be moving less than five miles without leaving the borough of Queens. Moreover, 'Our respect for tradition should be tempered by the fact that the five US championships have been united at Forest Hills for only eight years.' Allow me to patch together a few snippets from the rest of that valediction:

'The stature of the US championships was raised—and the strain on the West Side Tennis Club increased—by two events in the 1960s. One was the provision of charter flights to strengthen the draw by bringing over more leading players from Europe. The other was the advent of open competition. After that, things happened fast ... All the time, the crowds and the prize money were increasing. Those were exciting years. But in personal terms they became unpleasant. The worst features were the congestion, the litter, and the noise.

The litter arose largely from the excessive consumption of refreshments and the inadequate provision of garbage bins. The noise—well, just imagine a busy flight path, a railroad, a traffic-choked chunk of suburbia, police and fire sirens, salesmen at a string of concession booths, and the echoes from a clubhouse packed with diners and drinkers.

... Much of this cannot be escaped, even at Flushing Meadow, where a grand new tennis complex will embellish a run–down park that has had no consistent function since the 1964 World Fair. The noise and litter will doubtless stay with the tournament. But there will be more room for everyone—for their cars, too—and perhaps a few quiet corners for private dreams and memories. And when we think of Forest Hills, we shall select only the good books from the library of the mind—the tennis, the friends, and the bookstore and pizza parlour down the road.'

So in 1978 we moved over to the new national tennis center (sic) installed on 16 acres of a public park at Flushing Meadow.

The Olympia Brass Band, street musicians summoned from New Orleans, included the number 'Who's Sorry Now?' (a relevant question) in their programme for the opening ceremony. A jazz group has continued to welcome incoming customers to the finals. Another pleasing feature is the parkland beyond the center's peripheral fencing. The hard courts (an acrylic cushion on an asphalt base) are quintessentially American but tough on the feet and legs. The most obvious snag is the deafening roar of low-flying aircraft when they take off from runway 13 at La Guardia, little more than a mile away. And although Flushing Meadow is far more roomy than Forest Hills, access to the courts is no easier: and high court-side barriers permit only short-distance views. Oddly, the courts were not all laid in the same direction (as they are at Roland Garros and Wimbledon) and their somewhat haphazard numbering has made route-finding trickier than it might have been.

The two main courts, originally one huge arena, are divided by a towering structure that has raised the Press 81 ft above ground level. For a few years we reached this eyrie via an elevator, when it worked, or via 133 steps when it did not. Now there are two elevators and both work. The Press Box provides a bird's eye view of two courts and a panoramic prospect of the distant Manhattan skyline. But it is a long way from the tennis and has a glass front that takes the full glare of the afternoon sun—less welcome to working journalists than it might be to tomato plants. I often dictate articles while lying on the floor in the shade under the desk. Yes, they made mistakes at Flushing Meadow. But its ambience is in harmony with New York, whereas one often felt that Forest Hills was aspiring to mirror the qualities of Wimbledon and, to some extent, Roland Garros. Like it or not, Flushing Meadow is unashamedly American and has become a tennis Mecca for what they used to call 'the smart set'.

In 1978 Chris Evert became the second player (Helen Jacobs was the first) to win the women's singles championship for a fourth consecutive year and Jimmy Connors became the first man since Bill Tilden to contest five consecutive singles finals. Moreover, Connors completed the unique feat of winning the US title on three different surfaces: grass, shale, and hard courts. Neither of them, however, was mentioned in the first paragraph of my last report:

'The odd thing about the 1978 United States tennis championships is that whenever we take the memories off the shelf and clear away the dust, the dominant figures to emerge may be a girl who lost and a man who did not even play. The girl was Pamela Shriver, aged 16 years and two months, competing for the first time, who had to miss the first few days of a new school term because she became the youngest player to reach the women's singles final. The man, old enough to be her grandfather, was W. E. "Slew" Hester, president of the United States Tennis Association, whose initiative and tenacity made a mighty new tennis complex spring up in six months in the middle of New York. They had the nerve to believe these things were possible.'

In 1979 Tracy Austin, aged 16 years and nine months, became the youngest player to win the women's championship and John McEnroe, aged 20 years and seven months, became the youngest winner of the men's title since Pancho Gonzales in 1948. But the news story of the tournament was a midnight scandal that arose from the threat of a mob take-over. Because of an industrial dispute, *The Times* was not being published. This condensed account is taken from my report for *International Tennis Weekly*. Note the unusually racy style, which arose partly from the subject matter and partly because I was writing for a publication that is essentially American:

'The bottom line was that the disqualification of Ilie Nastase was rescinded not because of any procedural error by the umpire

---

or referee, but because the fans were dangerously angry ... John McEnroe beat Nastase 6–4, 4–6, 6–3, 6–2 in a three-hour match that produced the loveliest singles play of the week. With versatile shot-making they improvised some breathtaking rallies. But the fans wanted more than that from two anti-heroes who are not renowned for their composure or dignity.

It didn't help that this obviously combustible contest was scheduled for second match in the evening, a time when the inhibitions of many of the 10,549 spectators had been loosened by alcoholic juices. It didn't help that the crowd decided Nastase was their boy, that provocative anti-McEnroe barracking was part of the script. It didn't help that the fans were ignorant of the point penalty system and that no one explained it to them. It didn't help that Frank Hammond, the umpire, overplayed his own role in the drama like a bit-player trying to upstage the stars. He talked too much, made excessive use of the mike, and badgered Nastase as if dealing with an errant child. That angered the crowd. Hammond began to lose control of everything except the bedrock of umpiring procedure. This was sad. He is a fine umpire and a warm, charming man.

What brought the pot to the boil was Hammond's ultimate application of the point penalty system. With McEnroe serving at 2–1 in the fourth set, he was controversially granted a point for a service Nastase said he was not ready to return. Nastase protested and so—more clamorously—did the crowd. Hammond then awarded McEnroe the game. Thus began a 17-minute interruption enforced by wildly angry scenes. The din was almost terrifying: chanting, catcalls, boos, and the rest. The trash thrown on court included beer cans and cups. Fighting broke out in the crowd. An invasion of the court seemed imminent. Police and security men were summoned. Hammond—now reinforced by the referee, Mike Blanchard—appealed to the players to get the show on the road again because there seemed no other way of pacifying the public. But Nastase, 1–3 down, refused to serve. Finally, on Blanchard's instructions, Hammond "put the clock on him". Having allowed Nastase 58 seconds instead of the official 30, Hammond awarded game, set and match to McEnroe.

The tournament director, Bill Talbert, then decided that the threat of a riot was serious. He reckoned the only way to restore order was to overrule the Blanchard–Hammond decision, dismiss Hammond, and resume the match with Blanchard in the chair. Frank Smith, the grand prix supervisor, agreed ... One odd result of their decision was that it earned Hammond much more sympathy and respect than would have gone his way had the disqualification stood. The argument now concentrated not on his earlier deficiencies, but on the fact that he had taken a hazardously bold decision on the referee's instructions (in "putting the clock" on Nastase, the only remaining penalty at Hammond's disposal was disqualification) but had then had the rug pulled from under him by other officials.'

In 1980 there was limited success for an experiment with only six court officials, three of whom had to move about rather a lot. Bjorn Borg beat Roscoe Tanner in a match 'punctuated by as much nerve-twanging tension as a Hitchcock script'. The combination of aircraft noise and drifting aromas from the open-air food village once prompted me to write: 'This tournament does not tickle the senses: it assaults them.' There was a sensuous theme, too, in one's reaction to scheduling that sandwiched the women's singles final between the men's semi-finals. All three lasted for the maximum number of sets:

'There are times when life is too good to us, when the appetite is so sated that the gourmet becomes a gourmand and even the brandy loses its flavour. That was how it was on the penultimate day. We were given three singles matches, all of them delectably thrilling in their form and content and dramatic fluctuations. One would have been enough to satisfy most tastes. The second helping was welcome but not strictly necessary. The third was really too much. But that was how the television programme planners wanted it.'

The 100th anniversary of the men's singles and doubles championships coincided, in 1981, with the end of the Borg era. John McEnroe beat him in the Wimbledon and US finals in turn and within a few months Borg (additionally under official pressure to play more tournaments than he wanted to) announced that he had had enough. Borg had failed in 10 attempts to win the US title. By contrast McEnroe became the first man since Bill Tilden to be champion three years running. Tracy Austin won the women's singles for the second time in three years. As had been the case at Wimbledon a year earlier, the women's final was decided by a tie-break.

Martina Navratilova drew another blank in 1982, which meant that like Borg and hundreds of others she had failed in 10 attempts to win the title. But in 1983 she broke through at last—and never lost more than three games in any set. It was in 1983 that, one day, the efforts of reporters and broadcasters to communicate with distant audiences were drowned by the amplified rehearsal of a barber-shop quartet, who had taken over the main court during the interval between daytime and evening programmes. Things like that tend to happen at Flushing Meadow. And with three days to go I began my report thus:

'The United States championships begin to finish this morning. The men's doubles final will be played at 10.30. In both singles events, the semi-final and final rounds will be played on consecutive days, which should ensure that no player is quite at his or her best in the final. The tournament has mostly been played in daylight but on Sunday evening will probably end under floodlights.

This sounds, and is, ludicrous. Bob Howe, the referee, said

yesterday: "The biggest factor here is how much time you can get on CBS television. Everything works on the ratings and the higher ratings are from 4 p.m. onwards".'

Let me expand that. The men's singles final starts soon after four o'clock and, assuming it is a long match, travels on through twilight into floodlit darkness after a spectacular sunset over the Manhattan skyline. Such varying conditions are far from ideal. Note, too, that the practice of having separate daylight and flood-light programmes during the first 10 days cannot be equally fair to all players. And it asks too much of the players to contest singles semi-finals and finals on consecutive days just because that suits television. The women's final is scheduled between the men's semi-finals and consequently has no fixed starting time. Finally, the 90-second changeover limit is sometimes extended in order to accommodate television commercials. Much of that is farcical. Imagine the fuss there would be if the programme deliberately scheduled for the last three days at Flushing Meadow happened *by accident* at Roland Garros or Wimbledon. No wonder the championships have acquired such disparaging sub-titles as 'The CBS championships' and 'a TV Game Show'. No wonder I was once driven to write that the USTA 'continue to behave like highly paid lackeys of CBS television'. There is a case of sorts for evening tennis, catering for the needs of those with a day's work to do. Except for that, one can only suggest that the USTA are awash with revenue from television companies but, in order to get it, have compromised the tournament's integrity. Money talks, but must we always listen?

The 1984 tournament made a promising start:

'The United States championships are so boisterous, brash, and bizarre that the unusual is almost commonplace. Unless one's mind is in gear all the time, the absurd can easily escape notice. Take two incidents that cropped up yesterday while Flushing

Meadow was roasting under the heat of noon: a Swede munched Danish pastry in mid-match and a lady spectator was splattered when a tennis ball plunged into her cardboard beaker of Coca-Cola.'

The Swede was Anders Jarryd. The other incident occurred when a ball flew off the frame of Ivan Lendl's racket, soared into the terraces, and plopped into the beaker of Coke—a startling experience for the lady holding it, because she was looking elsewhere at the time. The Press had some fun, too. The overseas corps were often seen toting around cardboard boxes that looked like gasmask containers (if your memory goes back that far):

'Free enterprise has run riot. The company which formerly provided private lines and telephones has been shattered into a chaos of separate concerns. Now the lines come from one source, the telephones from a variety of others. Reporters have been scurrying about Manhattan to buy or rent telephones which they connect to the lines for the day's work. Then the telephones are packed away for safe keeping. In New York only the rich or the foolish leave saleable items lying around.'

British reporters were even more interested than usual in efficient communications. John Lloyd became the first British player to reach the last eight of the men's singles since Mark Cox in 1966:

'Nobody jokes any more about "Chris Lloyd's husband" or the "John Zaccaro" of tennis. He is a celebrity in his own right. Lloyd's film-star looks, engaging personality, and no-nonsense approach to tennis (and life as whole) pack in the customers whenever he goes on court.'

But I was sick at heart. Globe-trotting reporters (and players, for that matter) always hope that no domestic crisis will crop up when they are far from home. But such crises do crop up. My wife told me on the phone one day that our 10-year-old English and Gordon Setters had set about each other in an unstoppably violent 12 st dog-fight. The brave but arthritic English Setter looked like 'a chewed up rug' and was close to death. Somehow my wife and the vet kept him alive until I flew home. Then we fed him all the goodies he most enjoyed and I helped him to totter over a small segment of his favourite walk. I dug a grave watered with sweat and tears, in the spot the old boy seemed to have chosen—he used to sit under a yew high in our wood, looking over the valley. The vet called. And we laid that noble dog to rest.

In such circumstances wives always have the heavier load to bear. I had work to keep the mind occupied—and that was the year the scheduling achieved a crazy kind of splendour. The penultimate day's programme on the main court spanned more than 12 hours. Stan Smith beat John Newcombe in the over-35s final. Ivan Lendl saved a match point and beat Pat Cash in a five-set match that left everyone emotionally drained. Martina Navratilova beat Chris Lloyd in a three-set women's final. Then John McEnroe beat Jimmy Connors in another thrilling five-setter. That match ended at 11.13 p.m. Next day:

'At least John McEnroe and Ivan Lendl saved on the electricity bill—there was no need to switch on the floodlights—and gave us time for a leisurely farewell dinner amid the bustle of Runyon's. McEnroe took only an hour and 40 minutes to beat Lendl 6–3, 6–4, 6–1 in the men's singles final of the United States championships.

... McEnroe is the most gifted shot-maker since the more elegant but less sternly competitive Ilie Nastase. Lendl wrote humdrum prose while McEnroe wrote poetry—unfussy, but so carefully constructed that every word hit the mark.

... Both had been physically drained by awfully strenuous semi-finals. Lendl looked stiff—in body and mind, technique and tactics.

McEnroe's performance was exemplary in its economy of effort. His reactions were fast, his touch sure. He was aggressive but did not waste energy on brutality. Like a boxer intent on winning inside the distance, he made every punch count.'

In 1985 I changed hotels and discovered an odd by-product of Manhattan's attitude to security. On three consecutive mornings I had to telephone the porter and ask him to release me from a room that could not be unlocked from the inside. Maybe they thought I would leave town without paying the bill. Kevin Curren was not enjoying himself, either. He was beaten in the first round and promptly expressed his dislike for New York in general and Flushing Meadow ('They should drop an A bomb on it') in particular. In specifying the type of bomb he went too far. Then the storm hit us: 'Curren's revenge', as somebody put it. There was a mini-tornado ('tornadette'?) in the park next door and the tennis complex received the fringe benefits. Trees were felled, a marquee flattened, fences and awnings rearranged. Cascading water transformed the main court into a pool more than ankle deep. There were minor injuries, plus shock cases, and the premises were evacuated—except, that is, for the workers. Did I mention that the Press Box was 81 ft above ground level? Twice it swayed under the assault. This was confusing because by that time of day most of us had emptied the odd can of beer anyway. Some of the telephones ceased to function. And peering out through a pane of glass at an impenetrable sheet of whirling rain and hail was rather like a close-up view of an automatic washing machine (maximum revs).

A few days later Randy Gregson, the USTA president, invaded the colony of British reporters with the news that he had brought 'a friend' to see us. This turned out to be the Duchess of Gloucester, who happened to be in town. Conversation turned to the storm and I said it was a little unusual to tap away at a typewriter that was moving about. Whereupon John Parsons interjected: 'He's often *thought* it was moving ...' Well, not quite. But *The Times* does more than the *Daily Telegraph* to ensure full employment among brewers and vintners.

The Duchess eyed the unfinished prose in my typewriter—something to do with Ivan Lendl, Yannick Noah, and the 'CBS championships'. This, I explained, was the second story of the day: the Balmoral piece had already gone and I was now working on the Kensington Palace edition. While all this chit-chat was going on I noticed that our guest was wearing a brooch on which the initials 'B' and 'R' were intertwined, which caught the eye because I have a tie embroidered with the same initials. The royal version represents 'Birgitte' and 'Richard' rather than rhythm and blues. Some people, she said, thought it stood for British Rail.

Yes, definitely a fun person—and brave, too, because by that time of day the Press Box was reeking with the mingled flavours of tobacco smoke, beer, and sweat. It was one of those afternoons when the temperature was in the middle 90s and, down in the main amphitheatre, often exceeded 110. And the humidity was appalling. Flushing Meadow can be like an open-air sauna installed in a fairground next to an airport.

You want to know about the tennis? Well, Boris Becker did not get past the fourth round. Joakim Nystrom stopped him:

'These Swedes are delightful: fine sportsmen who get on with the job without fussing (except for Jarryd, who often seems close to a nervous breakdown) and talk about the game and themselves with no hint of either conceit or false modesty. The sleepiest of the lot is Nystrom, who beat Becker 6–3, 6–4, 4–6, 6–4 in two hours and 43 minutes on Monday evening and thus cancelled the Becker–McEnroe clash which many had assumed would be the match of the tournament.

Becker, aged 17, is learning his trade. It is extraordinary that so much should be expected of him so soon. For his age he has done remarkably well in the past nine months, reaching the last eight in Australia, winning Wimbledon, and advancing to the last

16 here. Should anyone—even Becker, an ambitious but sensible lad—be disappointed with a record like that?

... This was a useful match for Becker. One day he will probably contest the final here—and the men's final tends to span daylight, twilight, and floodlit night. All that happened on this occasion, too. Becker drank deeply from the wine of experience, which leaves an after-taste of wisdom.'

And a German teenager reached the singles semi-finals anyway. This was Steffi Graf, aged 16, who took two hours and 50 minutes to beat Pam Shriver 7–6, 6–7, 7–6 in an absorbing, awfully tough match. But the new women's champion was Hana Mandlikova, who thus terminated a sequence of 15 grand slam championships won by either Chris Lloyd or Martina Navratilova. On consecutive days Miss Mandlikova beat Mrs Lloyd 4-6, 6–2, 6–3 and Miss Navratilova 7–6, 1–6, 7–6:

'Miss Mandlikova was Australian champion in 1980 and French champion in 1981, but at that time she was too immature as a woman and too inconsistent as a player to consolidate her advance. Even so, in the absence of Tracy Austin and Andrea Jaeger she remained the most obvious threat to Mrs Lloyd and Miss Navratilova.

... A player with so many gifts was always capable of the occasional big win. The task of battling through seven matches to win a grand slam championship calls for something extra in the way of stamina and resilience, both mental and physical. For Miss Mandlikova all that came to fruition here. As a woman and as a player she has grown up to a point at which she can look adversity in the face without flinching, without looking for excuses, without any undue erosion of self-assurance ...'

Another Czechoslovak, Ivan Lendl, beat John McEnroe 7–6, 6–3, 6–4 in the men's final. The score was an accurate reflection of the way they played but McEnroe's moderate form was a condemnation of the congested scheduling. The previous day he had been put through the wringer by Mats Wilander in a semi-final that spanned three hours and 50 minutes of oppressive heat and humidity:

'On Sunday he won 13 of the first 14 points and led 5–2. Then Lendl saved a set point with a fierce forehand—and proceeded to blast McEnroe into submission with relentlessly powerful hitting. McEnroe hung on as best he could. But the pace and precision of Lendl's services, volleys and ground strokes never wavered—and in the last two games Lendl added the delicate flourishes of a top-spun lob on each flank.'

Ken Flach and Robert Seguso won the men's doubles amid a storm of controversy:

'Henri Leconte and Yannick Noah were within a point of leading by two sets to one when Leconte hit a forehand and Flach took evasive action. The shot went out. Flach has not denied that the ball may have touched him, as the Frenchmen insisted. But Flach did not offer an opinion. The point should have been replayed.

What matters now is that if the officers of the Association of Tennis Professionals can spare the time from administrative manoeuvres and their favourite toy, the rankings computer, they should remind members that tennis is a sport, that the conduct of professionals should be exemplary, and that any player who even suspects that a shot may have touched him should instantly say so.'

With that, the TV game show was over and it was back to Manhattan for a farewell dinner, Alaskan crab legs and white wine, at Hobeau's on 2nd Avenue. There was a storm at Kennedy and fog at Heathrow, so we spent 11 hours on the aircraft instead of seven, the unwelcome extension including a return trip between London and Prestwick. But that sort of thing is part of the job—a job you have been sharing with me since we first went to Paris together in 1960.

EPILOGUE

THIS 26-YEAR browse among the pleasures of Paris, Wimbledon and New York has inevitably been arbitrary in its choice of extracts, anecdotes, and comments on the writing trade. But the authentic flavour of the game's greatest festivals is fresh on the palate and will, I hope, linger there. We have looked at the places, the players, and the play through the eyes of that privileged minority, the reporting corps, for whom

> All the world's a stage,
> And all the men and women merely players:
> They have their exits and their entrances.

Nothing of outstanding importance has been neglected, not in terms of the three 'biggies' anyway. And I make no apology for laying bare a few preferences: for the craftsman rather than the drudge, for the self-disciplined sportsman rather than the petulant big-head; and for the French championships rather than their rivals. And how refreshing it is to come across players who manifestly enjoy playing tennis for a living, as distinct from the currently fashionable breed of po-faced efficiency experts. They talk about 'percentage' tennis: respecting the odds. That rule is a sound guide but a dull master. The spirit of adventure lies somewhere within all of us and, occasionally, demands discreet indulgence. Santana and Laver and Nastase and Panatta indulged it—and they won a few tournaments.

Some of the laughter has died. Today's players are too busy to

get to know one another and let their hair down as their predecessors did. Too busy rushing from one tournament to the
next. Too busy making money for themselves and dollar-oriented
management companies. Too busy trying to rise a few notches in
the computed rankings that decide who gains direct entry to the
big events. But today's harder attitudes have little to do with
professionalism per se: playing a game for money tests the character but does not change it. The circuit has simply become something of a treadmill. The system makes money but does not always
make sense.

The international circuit has become too predictably formal to
be consistently stimulating. It has an expanding bureaucracy and,
admirable though their motives may be, the bureaucrats are
imposing on the circuit an excessive, unhealthy uniformity. The
governing councils have acquired more power than is good for
the game. They have acquired it by outwitting independent or
formerly independent entrepreneurs who have been responsible
for most of the successful initiatives in modern professional tennis.
An example is the European Champions' Championship, an independent event promoted in Antwerp. Can this joyously spectacular
festival survive in a hostile climate or must it eventually submit—
as the World Championship Tennis events and Düsseldorf's World
Team Cup competition submitted— to the benevolent totalitarian
authority of the council who govern the grand prix circuit?

This is not to suggest that the independents should control the
game—merely that they should have a little more elbow room,
that all promoters should have more scope for initiative and
diversity in every aspect of tournament organization (format,
eligibility for entry, the prize money break-down, and so on). In
short, the game needs more freedom, less regimentation.

Yes, the tennis circuit has problems. But as Philippe Chatrier—
one of the more imaginative administrators—is fond of pointing
out, they are the problems of success and most other sports would
welcome them. And don't worry about the players. They are as

delightful as ever they were, with the reservation that they earn more and laugh less than earlier generations. Moreover, their reputations and market values depend, as they always did, on what they achieve in the three great championships and the fourth leg of the grand slam, in Melbourne.

Essentially, nothing has changed.